In the fall of 1994, 21-year-old Elena Nikitina disappeared. Drugged and kidnapped by a group of Chechen gangsters, she was taken to Chechnya and held in a tiny room. Through eight horrifying months of captivity, and the outbreak of a genocidal war, all that kept her alive was hope.

"This book will astonish and inspire you. One woman's shocking true story of abduction, war and survival." - Brian Whitney, author of SUBVERSIVE

"Elena's powerful, heart-wrenching story of inner strength in the face of impossible odds will change your life." - Patrick Quinlan, *Los Angeles Times* bestselling author of ALL THOSE MOMENTS and SMOKED.

"An amazing true story about a beautiful young women taken from her family, friends and everything she knew. This story shows that we don't really know how strong we can be until being strong is all we have." – Brenton Petrey

Dear Gregg,

I have started reading your book The Russian Hoax, and the political depth fascinates me. I would be honored if you could accept my book. Hope you will enjoy the read.

With love,
Elena

04. 28. 19

Girl, Taken

A true story of abduction, captivity and survival

Elena Nikitina

with Patrick Quinlan

ISBN: 0-9882138-6-9
ISBN-13: 978-0-9882138-6-9

For you, mama… For you, Ama…
For those who seek hope…

iliad Books

CONTENTS

The names and nicknames of criminals, and the names of some locations, were changed because the criminals were never caught.

ELENA NIKITINA

CHAPTER ONE

October 4ᵗʰ, 1994

I did not know where I was.

For a long time, I drifted in darkness. Then a thought came, unbidden.

I'm alive.

Another thought soon followed. Then another. They had a mind of their own, these thoughts. Gradually, they began to lead me up and out of the abyss.

They were confused, a mad jumble of images and ideas, and sensations and disembodied voices, all superimposed on each other. I recovered slowly, crawling through the buzz of a malfunctioning electrical wire that seemed to be inside my head. I felt how my lungs were filling with air; I began to do it consciously and with pleasure. I was breathing!

More clearly now I heard the revving of a car engine, and mingled with that, the sound of unfamiliar voices. Several men were speaking in a language I did not understand. My body, which had gone as limp and as soft as a fresh corpse, gradually began to stiffen and take form again. It twitched, then stretched, legs and arms lengthening – all of this as involuntary as the beating of my heart.

I tried to open my eyes. My eyelids seemed glued firmly shut until this point. They were so heavy it was almost unnatural to lift them.

In the first moments, my vision was out of focus. It was like a photograph taken at night, through a rainy, foggy window. Everything was smeared and hazy and very dark. But with each successive moment of consciousness, my wounded brain began to put all the puzzle pieces together. Soon enough, the picture became clearer – resolving itself, slowly and inexorably, into something I did not want to see.

I yearned to dive back to the darkness, the unconsciousness, back to where I was not able to feel the fear. But it was too late. I was awake now, becoming alert, and unable to retreat from reality.

I found myself in a car full of strangers, driving through the night.

Inky darkness flew along outside my window, shadowy landscapes passing formless and empty. The rickety car moved too quickly over rutted and pitted roads, shuddering and banging the entire time. I could make out nothing about where I was. The car seemed to be passing through an unpopulated countryside – there were no lights out there at all. Inside the car, a dim yellow dashboard light was on. The light cast a reflection on the window – showing me a distorted funhouse version of the men I was too afraid to look at directly.

I was in the back seat of a car being driven away from my life. The full horror of it began to sink in.

What has happened?
Where are they taking me?
Who are these men?

My body had gone numb from the uncomfortable position I was in, and instinctively I moved again. Now I noticed my tongue. It felt thick in my mouth.

I produced a sound, like a shout, but also like horrible animal groaning.

The men ignored me. They were talking incessantly. Their language seemed to me like the language of a lost jungle tribe. I rolled my eyes from side to side, trying to understand. Impenetrable darkness made it impossible to see their faces, but there were definitely four of them: a driver and three others. To my right, two passengers were squeezed in the back seat next to me.

My body was still under the influence of some kind of poison. My head felt like it weighed a ton, and my tongue refused to listen to my commands. It groaned again.

I grew more alert. The unconsciousness, fatigue and stiffness faded, leaving open a place for an increasing sense of all-consuming fear. At my left side, there was nothing but darkness. It sapped my confidence and my hopes. The idea struck me like an arrow – they had taken me. No one knew where I was.

Will these men rape me?

Will they sell me into slavery?
Will they kill me?

* * *

The last thing I remembered was the fight with my boyfriend. I argued with him and then I decided to go home.

It happened at night, three weeks past my 21st birthday.

That night, there was a party at the restaurant across the alley from my home. The restaurant was called Corvette, the newer place in town where my friends and I had parties all the time. It was a sweet, romantic time of life, and Corvette was our place.

It was a typical Russian hangout for young people. Loud, alive, buzzing, full of smoke and strong drink. The inside, true to its name, was decorated like a battle cruiser from the days of sailing – it looked like a pirate ship on the high seas – complete with rope rigging hanging along the walls, portholes, crossed swords, and deck cannons.

The restaurant was crowded that night, tables full of beautiful young people, drinking and talking and laughing and shouting. They were beautiful, and I was beautiful.

I can still see Sergey's angry face as we argued. He was a handsome guy, and I loved him in that way people love each other when they are 21. Intensely. Gigantically. Our love was all consuming. It was so huge, it was impossible. It was the biggest thing on planet Earth.

How could the world go on if Sergey and I were to break up? It must stop, at least for a moment, to acknowledge with its own heavy heart the passing of a relationship so beautiful that the poets would weep to think of it.

Yes, our love was like that.

Sergey was a sportsman. He was a boxer, and his training made him thin and strong, and vital, and full of energy. It was as if a current of electricity was passing through his body at all times. We made an attractive couple, and we enjoyed that about ourselves. We were made for each other.

If our love was gigantic, then so was our anger. It was anger appropriately sized to a love as enormous, and emotions as powerful, as ours. In my memory, Sergey's hazel eyes are on fire. He is yelling at me, but I am so angry, I can no longer hear what he is saying. All I can hear is the laughter and celebration all around us. All I can see is the color red. Sergey is gesturing with his long arms, like a great bird, a crane, but even as he flaps his wings, he fades from my view, backward into the cigarette smoke and the red haze of my anger.

5

I felt a sudden urge to leave the party. I had to get away. The first floor apartment that I shared with my mother was just steps from there. I wanted to escape the ugliness of the fight, escape the self-important flightless birdlike flapping of my boyfriend, escape the god-awful smoke and the cacophonous noise of the merrymakers, and exchange it all for the warm hugs of my mama and the quiet coziness of our flat.

"I'm leaving," I told Sergey.

He dismissed me with a violent flap of his wing. For a second, he reminded me not of a bird, but of a symphony conductor contemptuously demanding a crescendo from a third rate orchestra. "Do whatever you want, I'm staying."

He turned away from me, and I moved toward the door. I left the restaurant.

I was wearing a little black dress, my favorite piece of clothing. It was so tight and sexy, it fit like a second skin, like the skin of a snake. As I walked, the dress treacherously tried to ride up, exposing my already barely covered legs. In the doorway of the restaurant, I pulled the hem of the dress down and stepped outside.

The long boulevard was empty. Everything was quiet, and the alley was dark. In my youth, the nights were always dark.

I started walking, in a hurry to get home. I needed probably ten steps, maybe a couple more than that with my high heels on, to reach the corner of the building and then make a right turn to enter the front dooryard.

"This dress again!"

It was my favorite. I loved that dress, and as much as I loved it, I also hated it because it always rode up when I walked. I stopped for a second to fix it. I pulled the hem of the dress down with both hands, took a step and fell into sudden darkness.

* * *

My body was fighting off the remnants of whatever drugs they had used on me. The car, rushing on the off-roads, shook me so hard that the poison was jolted out of my body, and soon I finally came to my senses. One thing I knew for sure – my old life was over and something new had begun, something which had no explanation yet, something that I could not change.

I saw myself trapped, enslaved.

I had to speak. I had to say something to them. They had made a mistake. They had taken the wrong person. I had to tell them. My mind woke completely. My soul wanted to howl like a wounded wolf. I suddenly heard my own voice.

"Who are you?" I said. "What do you want?"

The man in the front passenger seat turned around to face me. I recognized him! Everyone called him the Italian. I did not know his real name.

He was a Chechen, and he was handsome. He was tall, and wore fashionable clothes for the times. His long dancer's legs were wrapped in tight jeans. He looked great. He had suddenly come down to Astrakhan from Moscow and started hanging out at Corvette and other places my friends and I went. People said he had lived in Rome sometime before. That's why they called him the Italian.

He had first appeared in September, just before my birthday. He seemed to show up everywhere we went. I thought it was a pleasant coincidence. "Oh, there's the Italian again." Our eyes would meet and we would exchange a few words. I found him attractive. In those days, I was learning to give men sultry looks and seductive smiles. I tried a few out on him.

In the car, the Italian was looking at me, only now the glamor was gone – his once contagious smile had turned into a hideous grin. Seeing him there, I went speechless again, this time not from the toxic substances, but from astonishment bordering on shock.

In the dim light of the tiny bulb above the windshield, I could finally see the *real* face of the Italian. It no longer seemed attractive – on the contrary, its perfect features seemed disgusting.

He sat there half-turned and looking at me. He did not answer my questions, but simply grinned with his crooked smile. The tip of his sharp nose raised upwards. His eyes shone, even in the darkness, whether from the alcohol, drugs or from the newly acquired power he had over me. He was still in the same clothes he had been wearing in the restaurant.

I was in the same clothes, too. I noticed now that I was only missing my high heeled shoes – I felt the unpleasant texture of a rubber mat under my feet. All of a sudden, I began to feel cold. My whole left side ached from being in the same position for a long time, pressed against the car's cold door.

A sudden attack of fear surged within me. *I can't do this! I do not want to go anywhere with these people!*

I wanted to go home. I wanted to go back. My heart was beating at a furious pace, and the blood pounded inside my temples.

My hands were not restrained – they simply hung on both sides of my body. My left arm was numb and frozen. I tried to move and change my position, but the small car's backseat was not designed for three passengers. I was pressed against the door at an awkward angle. The man sitting to my right pushed his huge elbow into my side – he was too big for the car.

Outside, it was still dark. I could not see the big man's face – only his stooped profile and his nose, bouncing up and down on the bumps with the car, which was still speeding along the back roads. Unanswered questions in my head mixed with an overwhelming sense of fear and helplessness.

I did not know what to do. I did not know what to say so they would let me go.

I felt all my strength coming back – maybe I could jump out of the car and run away, run to where there was no car, and no people like these. Or maybe this was a nightmare and if I jumped out, I would just wake up.

As my eyes became accustomed to the dark, I took a quick look at the door. I tried to figure out the handle to open it and then jump out. I decided I'd rather be smashed under the car's tires than stay inside another minute.

There was something wrong with the door. It had no cover on it. In the darkness, I could distinguish wires within the open panel. All the insides were visible and welded to each other, or maybe wrapped in something – it was hard to say. There seemed to be nothing I could simply pull which would open the door. It made me want to scream in frustration.

Everyone in the car was silent now. The only sound was the car's engine, which roared like a tractor.

Someone said something I did not understand. Maybe they were speaking in Chechen, since the Italian was a Chechen.

Was he really a Chechen?

I realized I knew nothing about him, only rumors and hearsay. He could be anyone from anywhere. Fear and despair took possession of me completely. I wanted to run away so badly, to run away and forget all of this. I wanted out.

"I need to go to the bathroom," I said. Nobody seemed to pay attention.

What if they don't speak Russian?

But it couldn't be. I knew for sure that the Italian spoke Russian.

"I need to go to the bathroom," I said again.

The man behind the wheel said something in the foreign language. The Italian pulled a bottle from his jacket. To me, it looked like a bottle of a liquor, filled with a dark liquid. The Italian stretched out his arm and handed me the bottle:

"Drink it."

I knew that he spoke Russian! I'd heard him speak it a few times. His Russian was pretty good, with a subtle accent.

His eyes sparkled at me again. He looked like a demon.

I did not want to put their foul poison in my body.

I shook my head. "I won't."

The giant man who was just sitting quietly to my right all this time suddenly turned towards me, and with only his left arm, he pressed my entire body against the seat. He rested his elbow in my solar plexus, his gigantic palm gripping my still numb left hand. He was so huge and heavy that I felt my bones cracking underneath the weight of his arm, as if they were caught in a vise. I could not move – his hand was like a massive clamp. Everything was happening so fast, I could not figure out what was going on.

The man held down my weak body with his terrible strength, and at the same time, he opened my mouth with his other hand, compressing my cheeks together, his fingers painfully pushing into my skin. The Italian stretched back from the front seat, held the bottle above my head, and poured the alcohol into my mouth – it burned like wildfire.

The big man's elbow pressed my stomach so hard, I thought I would burst. I could barely breathe – the flaming liquid fell onto my tongue and flowed down my throat. I was going to suffocate. I tried to resist and set my head free, but the man only tightened his vise grip on my face. And I growled, wildly, through the pouring liquid.

"I'll do it!"

The clamps let me free. The massive arm snaked away. I started to breathe again, and my twisted face went back to its normal shape. My throat and mouth were on fire but I felt a little warmer inside. I wiped the spilled liquor from my face.

"I'll do it myself."

I spoke it with all the hatred I could muster. I snatched the bottle from the Italian, and took a long sip. I needed a drink. The nasty liquid ran into my throat, burning, but warming me from the inside. I liked the sensation it gave me. I took a few more sips, one after another after another, until I felt like I was going to throw up. A surge of heat suddenly enveloped me like a cozy blanket. I felt even warmer than before. The voices faded and started drifting somewhere far away. I felt much better. I don't know if I managed another sip – the waves were already carrying me into the safe darkness. Again.

October 5^{th,} 1994
Astrakhan, Russia

The woman always believed in premonitions, dreams and other magic.

She was almost used to it – many times, an otherworldly, unknowable force had informed her of something that later came to pass. And now a new feeling surged through her, as persuasive as any she had ever experienced, and so strong that it commanded her full attention. For a few seconds, she could not move – the feeling penetrated to her core.

Disaster had struck.

She leaned with her forehead against the cool glass of the apartment window. The feeling of helplessness was like two strong hands, squeezing her throat with incredible force. She realized exactly what it was, or rather *who* it was, that caused her such foreboding. At that moment she knew for sure:

Her immensely beloved daughter Lena – she was gone.

Thoughts raced through her mind: *What to do? Run to the police right now and report a premonition?* Only an idiot would do such a thing – no one would believe her. Her only choice was to wait – and to pray – maybe this time her vision would not come to pass.

"Please, God… *Please.*"

Behind the glass pane of the window, the street grew dark as night came. She could barely distinguish a few far away stars. The time passed slowly, and her heart thumped fast and loud, so loud she could hear it. The surrounding air, it seemed, was saturated with the banging of drums and the clanging of bells, all of it coming from the desperate beating in her own chest.

Outside, the night descended into jet-black darkness. Her apartment became dark, and she was left alone with her dark thoughts. She knew it now beyond doubt:

Lena will not be home tonight – something terrible has happened.

The woman sat up all night in her living room chair, watching the shadows and waiting, until the first light peeked inside her windows, bringing with it a bleak and dreary day. She rose from her chair with difficulty – it seemed as if a heavy weight pressed her down.

She walked the early morning city streets to the police station. They brought her to a detective with beefy hands and the swollen, bulbous nose of a man who had downed too much vodka. The officer listened, but didn't seem concerned. He replied with an indifferent shrug of his shoulders:

"Don't worry. I'm sure she'll show up tomorrow. You know, we were all young once. If she doesn't return in three days, then come and see us again. We only accept missing person applications after three days."

Back home, the woman called Sergey. Maybe her daughter had stayed at her boyfriend's place, and they just fell asleep.

The woman's intestines were tied in knots as she waited for Sergey to answer his telephone.

She barely let him speak.

"Is she there? Is Lena with you?"

"No," he said. "I'm sorry. She's not here. We had an argument at the restaurant, and she went home alone."

The woman called all her daughter's friends. Had they seen her? No. No one knew where she was.

The woman stared at the phone. Her mind was not working. It was impossible to come up with a plan for further action. It was hard to think at all. She was left, alone in a room, with the ruthless feeling of loss. She wanted to howl in grief and helplessness.

CHAPTER TWO

October 1994
Grozny, Chechnya

I woke up for a little bit into blurriness and then fell into a dream again. I was immersed in some other world – a world without pain or thoughts, without feelings or experiences. I drifted. I felt like an abandoned ship without a helmsman, floating with the tides and blown about by the wind.

They kept me in a small room now.

I was drifting in darkness. The waves of oblivion covered me for long periods of time, an infinity of time, and then they were replaced by a fleeting surge of conscious existence, but only for a moment. I floated in a black eternity. I passed out of time and space, and I was forgotten. I even forgot myself. Then I came back again.

This endless and emotionless chain repeated in a circle – I don't know for how long. Maybe it happened that way, or maybe it was just my sore brain playing evil tricks on me. My mind refused to work in the usual mode. What was the reason for this? Was I in shock, or was I still being drugged? I had no idea.

In those moments, I did not understand that I should enjoy this vegetable existence and these blunted feelings. Later in my captivity, I became so desperate I would have given almost anything to escape into the black world of dreams, at least for a few moments, and forget where I was. Such lost lucidity was a gift rather than a punishment. Being numb meant there was no chance for tears, and terror, and impotent fury at my helpless state. Brief glimpses of consciousness alternating with bottomless sleep left no room for painful emotions.

After a couple of hours or couple of weeks (or perhaps it was years, or decades or centuries - time had lost all meaning), new people came for me. Even through my dreams, I realized that they wanted to take me with them. They were alien to me – men with blurred faces, framed by dark hair and beards. I did not understand what they were saying, and I did not care – I was beyond caring. I felt myself floating in the air like a balloon – so light and indifferent.

I was broken.

I was no longer me, not a full person, a mere shadow of the Lena I had been very recently.

I could no longer feel my senses, and could not be left on my own. I did not belong to myself. I could not make decisions: my life was decided by strange and scary people. I did not even know what would happen to me from one minute to the next. I was heavily intoxicated, whether by drugs or by fear, I couldn't tell. I could not resist anything. I could not say anything. I don't remember speaking at all.

Who are they?

What do they want?

In my rare moments of enlightenment these questions were raised over and over in my mind. I could not find an answer.

One of the blurry faces spoke to me in Russian. In my memory, his voice seems to echo from afar.

"We're moving," he said.

Was I hallucinating? The men in that place all seemed to have the same facial features. They were just blank faces, washed out, pixilated, devoid of any specific characteristics, as if they did not have faces at all.

The dark framing of their hair and their thick beards made their heads seem disproportionately large. They were Bobblehead men, men with gigantic heads, and faces that all looked identical.

I was out of the bedroom now, and present in that strange place as an invisible observer.

It seemed like I was the victim of some kind of joke, or hoax, or absurd game. Suddenly, the darkness enveloped me again. But this new darkness was different. It was not the kind of darkness into which you fall instantly, and disappear into a deep abyss. It was not the kind of darkness which draws you away so suddenly that it does not give you a chance to get scared for even a split second. It was not the same kind of darkness that I had already experienced.

This time it was such a darkness that regardless the effect of the drugs, you still feel the excruciating fear deep inside your brain. It was a darkness where you realize that the worst is just moments or even seconds away. It was the kind of darkness the condemned man experiences when he is brought to the scaffold to be executed. It was *that* kind of darkness.

They had covered my head with a black hood or sack.

One of the men carried me. I felt myself become like some boneless deep sea creature, a jellyfish, but a jellyfish made of bread dough, malleable and light. My breathing slowed down, my heart was barely beating, my muscles became limp and formless, and my body was slung over someone's shoulder like a bag of rice.

I knew it was the end.

Then there was a car, the road, and I was sprawled on the back seat with my face uncovered. And we were driving once again, driving through the night.

* * *

I woke up after a dream with the feeling that I had slept for ages.

Just before I opened my eyes, a thought flashed in my brain, like lightning. For a fraction of a second, it seemed like I had the answer. None of this was real. None of it had happened. There were no kidnappers. There was no rickety car. I had fallen asleep and it was all some kind of strange nightmare. In another second I would open my eyes and find myself right where I belonged - snug in my bed in the cozy apartment I shared with my mom.

I was wrong. My eyes popped open and confirmed the horrible truth. Everything that I hoped was a nightmare was in fact reality. Surprisingly, and sadly, my mind was crystal clear and in no way clouded...

I found myself in an unfamiliar room immersed in twilight. On one dark wall, I could make out a slightly lighter square where there was a window, tightly draped with something dark. But even through the gloom I could clearly discern its shape, because of a small amount of daylight penetrating along the edges of the window. In here, it was night. Outside, it was daytime.

To my right there was a wall with a carpet hung on it. This is a typically Eastern tradition. People hang thick, beautiful, colorful Turkish wool rugs on their walls. But this rug wasn't thick, and it wasn't beautiful. It was a cruel mockery of the tradition. The rug was thin, shabby, threadbare, hanging on nails hammered into the wall, a piece of woven fabric. It was like the flag of a ruined nation. A carpet maker would weep to see it, and my face was so close to the wall that I could see the rug's braids.

The room was like a loud scream in my face. Everything in it told me that the frightening episodes I remembered were not a dream. The memories treacherously started to arise, one after another, like shards of glass from a broken mirror, sharp painful pieces of the things that had happened to me. I could see it all. The moments marched through my head, one by one, like fascist shock troops. A lump formed in my throat, and each memory caused that lump to swell. Soon the lump was so fat, so thick, it would not let me to breathe.

This was not a dream. This was not a nightmare. It had all really happened, and it was still going on! For the first time, I was of sound mind and I finally realized the depth of my predicament.

I lay motionless, paralyzed with despair. Tears flowed from my eyes, across the cheeks and slipping like cool jets all the way down my neck. Fear and helplessness tied me down. I felt choked, like big strong hands were on my throat. My heart was torn apart. I lay on the bed and I could not move. Most of all, in that moment, I wanted to go back to sleep and never wake up.

I did not know how much time has passed since I was stripped of my former life, and now it seemed that it was a long time ago.

What's next? What could possibly be next?

I lay there and sobbed silently. I did not know why I was there, and I did not know what would happen to me. In my mind, I howled in agony, like a wounded animal. I shrieked in despair. But in the real world, I did not utter a sound. I wanted to be quiet, so as not to bring attention to myself. It was terrible to be here, but I suspected that by making noise, I could bring something even worse.

After some time, I got up slowly and sat on the bed. In the dim light I could see the poor interior of the premises. In the 1950s and 1960s, Nikita Khrushchev had sought to reform and improve housing across the Soviet Union. This room was the result – a small drab square, a utilitarian box. It won zero points for style. It was a standard room, one of millions like it, in millions of standard compact apartments, in hundreds of thousands of five-story buildings spread across the largest country on Earth. It was a triumph of function over form. It was ruthlessly efficient. Draw one box, then build it again and again and again.

I was on a wooden bed, and the bed was pushed up against the same wall that was curtained with that incomprehensible colored scrap of rug, that embarrassment to carpet makers and carpet traders everywhere. Under the only light spot – the window – there was a bedside table with an old cassette player. And that was the room – bed, window, table.

I sat up in bed. I was barefoot and my feet made contact with the cold floor. On the ground, a few feet away, I spotted a carelessly dropped pair of thin flat shoes, pink with white trim.

Hmmm, I've seen those before.

They were like an uncovered clue. A piece of my dream, a small detail which I had forgotten, had just been recalled. It made the nightmare even more real. I knew these slippers. I had already worn them in the previous place.

I slipped my feet into the cool insides of the shoes and got out of bed. My mouth was dry, my head was spinning, and I felt myself light and empty inside.

When was the last time I ate?

I've always been skinny, and I would constantly watch my diet and starve myself from time to time to stay fit. I still had my black dress on, rolled up high to the hips, almost to my waist line, showing the black lace panties I wore underneath. I stood up and dress easily dropped down my hips. Our relationship had changed. It seemed to me that it was no longer fitted to my body, as it had been before. Once it had hugged my curves, and now it was just hanging down, a black tube to cover myself with.

I lose weight quickly, and I obviously had not eaten for at least a couple of days. The little black dress had always been my favorite – it was like a sleeveless turtleneck, and it came to the mid-thigh. It fit me perfectly in all the right places. When I wore it with my black patent-leather high heeled shoes it looked… impressive, let's say. Impressive is a word, and so is sexy.

And that's how it looked. In my previous life, anyway.

Now, on top of my dress I wore a huge floor-length robe. I had no idea where it came from. It was one of those heavy velour robes that flooded the street markets and were sold by Vietnamese street vendors. It seemed that the robe was bright pink once, made of thick plush fabric and embroidered with various colors. Now it was old, and even in the dim light I could see that it was faded and frayed. Some unknown person had taken pity on me and draped me in the robe at some point.

When had that happened? While I was sleeping in the bed? In the car? In the other apartment? I didn't know.

Why am I here?

I couldn't understand it. Most of my life I had been a nice person. I had never done anything wrong. I didn't deserve to be punished like this. I tried to think of the worst thing I had done, something that might bring this terrible fate upon me.

One day, in the 6th grade, my girlfriend and I stole two bananas from the grocery store. It was the only store in the neighborhood that sold vegetables and fruits, and it was a place where once a year they sold bananas.

Bananas! They were the dream of every Soviet child – ripe, with little brown spots on their bright yellow skin, and a tropical fragrance, so foreign and sensual and so totally intoxicating. People would wait for them to arrive at the store for a full year, and then stand in a long line to buy just a few of them. I enjoyed that unusual exotic flavor, savoring every bite.

In Soviet times, bananas were not just some regular imported fruit – they were messages sent from another world, a place which the Soviet people were forbidden to enter. People would stand all afternoon in a long line not necessarily because they liked the taste of bananas. They would patiently wait just to get a small taste of the outside world.

That evening, my friend and I went to the vegetable shop to buy, as we often did, two glasses of delicious birch juice. We had a couple coins in our pockets that were given to us by parents. And there we were, standing in the tiny store, two sixth graders, in front of the huge glass showcase where the sellers displayed the grim, wilted and uninviting fruits and vegetables that were usually on offer.

But this day, things were different. On top of the showcase there were a few trays loaded with bright yellow bananas. It seemed like they must have been delivered to the store just a few moments before. No one was around. There was no line of people. In fact, there was not a single creature in the whole store – only us, two small children, staring up at that big bunch of long-awaited fruit and inhaling that smell, a smell that would drive a child mad.

We had a few coins in our pockets. But the money was not enough to buy the bananas. The money wasn't enough to buy even half of a single banana. But the bananas were *right there*. Their beauty beckoned to us, and that smell! It was the scent of mystery and adventure, of overseas and unknown countries.

We could just about reach up and touch them with our hands...

I think, by nature, the man is a very rotten creature. We are thieves and liars and murderers. We are con artists. We are dishonest with everyone, and most of all with ourselves. If there were not the harsh limits of the law and the threat of subsequent punishment, the world would quickly turn into a bloody mess. It would become chaos literally overnight, with people killing and hurting each other everywhere you look.

We were never taught to steal, and we knew that you are not supposed to take what is not your own. I don't remember saying a word to my friend, or she to me. There was a tray of individual bananas, which had been torn from the bunches in the process of transportation.

Our hands reached out with lightning speed. We grabbed one banana each and instantly disappeared from the store. We ran away as fast as we could, holding our sweet trophies.

We ran until we couldn't breathe. We hid inside a construction site, and after our wind came back, we ate the bananas. Mine was the sweetest and the most delicious banana I had ever tasted. I knew what it could cost me – a trip to the child's room at police station, a stark light shining in my face, and half a dozen stern-faced KGB men surrounding me.

Now, the banana faded from memory. The dark walls of the room, the gray and cold floor, the wooden bed, that improbable piece of old rug on the wall, the bedside table with a tape recorder on it – this was the dismal theater set of my surroundings. If I were in an existential play, one which took place entirely in a grim and unhappy room, they couldn't have designed it any better.

The door to the connected room was closed, and I did not want to open this Pandora's box. That door filled me with dread. It loomed there, threatening to open at any moment. I decided not to go out of the room voluntarily – I wanted to prolong my safe existence in this room.

I had been gone from home for some time. A day, two days, two weeks, it could have been any of these. And I realized now that the search for me had already begun. My mom would be pulling all the strings she had.

I just needed to sit tight and not to show my captors that I woke up, and just wait. I did not know where I was and what exactly had happened. I tried to restore the chain of events: a night out at the restaurant, then a fight with my boyfriend. Right now, from this room, the fight seemed so pointless, so dumb. After that, the rest was a blur – a car driving through the long night, the evil face of the Italian, foreign people talking in strange language, and then another car. Now this place.

It seemed like an eternity had passed since I last saw my loved ones.

* * *

I looked at the door again.

It was an ordinary door, painted gray.

I absolutely did not know what to do. Should I knock on the closed door and beg for mercy, cry and have a fit of hysterics?

Or should I just sit quietly and wait? Wait for what? Waiting is always the worst, but it still seemed better than the alternative. This strange prison cell of a room was bad enough. I was afraid to find something even more horrible behind that door.

I was exhausted from all the stress, overwhelmed with endless fear – I could not adequately think. I just sat quietly on the bed and looked around the room.

The color of the window bothered me. It was too dark. It was more than strange. I did not want to approach the window and take a closer look at it. I did not want to move for fear of making a noise – the floorboards could squeak under my feet.

Time passed, and the room did not get any brighter. A bare light bulb hung from the ceiling. Probably, I could turn the light on, but I was not going to do it. I was not going to do anything to bring the attention of whoever or whatever was behind that door.

It was a small-sized room, like those in many Soviet apartments, maybe 12 feet by 12 feet. It was spare and barren – it didn't seem like anyone lived there permanently. The wall was covered in nondescript wallpaper – grayish, damaged, scratched and spotted in places. The cheap bed was pushed up against the wall – it was narrow, with a thin wooden headboard and footrest. In the dim light everything looked gray – the sheets, the pillows, the quilt – everything.

I watched the door.

Even in the gloom, I could see the contrast of the dark circle of the built-in lock below the handle. That door separated me from the rest of the world - the world that was now turned into something wrong and pointless, ridiculous and absurd. Totally unnatural, like the sudden death of a newborn child.

I did not want the door to open.

Still, I was thirsty and my bladder had awakened. I couldn't hold it much longer. The state of the stress blunted the physiological needs of the body and kept them shut off for a while, but that had its limits, too. I was nauseated from hunger, I was thirsty, and I needed to use the bathroom – all at the same time.

I knew what I had to do. I had to stand up, step toward the door, and open it. But I couldn't do it. I was too scared. The very idea of opening that door flooded my system with adrenaline. My heart started thumping in my chest, and the throbbing in my head seemed like it would crack my skull into pieces. I did not know what I would say when the door opened. And what if it didn't open? Would I knock on it?

I couldn't bear it much longer – I needed to go to the bathroom! What if the door never opened and I had to go right here in the room? No! Please! I could not bear the shame...

My bladder was now on the verge of explosion. I had to do something.

Ugh. Why was THIS making me get out of the room, and head into the unknown? Why should I leave my safe room just because of my bladder?

I had sat on the edge of the bed the whole time after I woke up trying to be motionless. Now I hesitantly stood up, and wrapped the weird pink robe around my body, like it could defend me from something. With a pounding heart I moved towards the door. My heartbeat was so loud that it seemed to fill the whole empty room. If a person existed on the other side of that door, he could probably hear my heart, too.

The room behind the door was silent. For a brief moment, I had a new fear – there would be no one there, the door would be locked, I would be stuck in this room, and I would die of a bladder rupture in a pool of my own urine. I pushed the handle down, and indeed the door was locked. But immediately I heard someone behind the door moving towards it. My heart sank into my toes. I felt like I might vomit, if only there were food in my stomach. A key turned in the lock. Each turn of it echoed like a hammer banging on the anvil of my brain.

The door opened.

The first thing I saw was an automatic rifle that hung across a man's chest, with the barrel pointing to the side and the gun's strap around the man's thick tree trunk neck. After a moment of shock, I saw the man himself. I could not guess at his age. He was tall, with deep-set eyes on either side of a huge thick beak of a nose. He had dark hair, bushy and unkempt, and his beard was rather short, disheveled, and stuck out in different directions – as if it was made of wire and glued onto his massive chin. His head seemed disproportionately large. His arm rested on the barrel of his rifle, which was strapped on so high, it was almost to his chin. The gun seemed so natural on him it was almost as if he was born with it attached.

I only had one single desire – to get to the bathroom. I couldn't think about anything else. I was not even afraid of this man – I did not care. He held the door open with one hand. He looked at me without emotion. He was totally calm.

"I need to go to the bathroom," I said.

The man said nothing. I knew he understood me, because he jerked his head to the side, indicating the way to the toilet. He took a step back and let me come out, then immediately positioned himself in front of me. So I followed him to the bathroom.

It took no more than five or six steps. First we passed through a bigger room, then down a narrow corridor. In the hallway there were two white painted doors, with dark dirty spots and scratches on them. The door to the left was the kitchen. The door to the right was down a tiny hallway. It was the exit, the way out of here. Although both doors were closed, I knew what lay behind them.

In fact, I knew the layout of such apartments by heart. It was the typical for the ones built during the Khrushchev and Brezhnev eras of the Soviet Union, and I had been in places like this many times. When I was a teenager, we lived in a small military town, and our apartment was exactly the same.

The man brought me to the bathroom and then stood right behind me. I opened the door and rushed into the long-awaited paradise. The tiny room closed me in, affording me a small sense of privacy. The toilet room was not the cleanest place in the world. It was tiny, maybe three or four feet across. The walls were painted dark green. There was nothing in it except the toilet – not even any toilet paper. The toilet itself was gross, disgusting, like a public toilet at a bus station. There was a dark circle of rust inside the bowl, and yellow spots of urine along the edges. This was a place for men – widely understood to behave like barnyard animals in the absence of women.

Fortunately for me, the toilet still had the seat attached, a small miracle in itself. The seat was still where it belonged, and it was raised. It was probably the same seat that had come with the apartment when it was new – the standard Soviet toilet seat made of yellowish-brownish cork – a very practical color because the dark hue makes it hard to tell how filthy the seat really is. I lowered the seat very fast, trying to minimize the amount of time my fingers spent touching it.

I immediately sat on top of it, and experienced the absolute bliss, the sweet blessed relief caused by the release of my bladder. I suddenly realized that I hadn't showered in what felt like ages.

I felt so dirty.

The toilet room was separated from the bathroom proper, as in many of the old Soviet-era apartments. I wanted to wash my hands very badly. I wanted to wash my entire body. I pulled up my panties, flushed, and came out. My guard was leaning back against the wall like a statue. His epic bulk blocked the tiny hallway that led to the exit.

"Can I wash my hands?"

He nodded again, this time indicating the next door.

The bathroom was also painted dark green. It contained an old bathtub – someone had messily sealed the edges of it with concrete – a sink with bare pipes, and three strange vessels under it on the floor, probably to catch the water leaking from the bottom. A small rectangular piece of mirror on the wall completed the interior.

I opened the cold water tap and began to greedily drink from the stream, filling my body with life-giving moisture. I drank like someone who had just crawled across a blazing desert, a madwoman, desperate, dehydrated, and parched like the sun-baked ground. After I took in all I could, I brushed my teeth using my finger.

When I looked up, I saw a haggard face in the little piece of mirror. For a moment, I did not know the face as myself. It seemed like the face of an old person, or a witch. There were dark circles under the eyes. It might be smeared mascara from my long-ago night out in the restaurant, or it might be traces of dirt and dust, mingled with exhaustion. My once-shiny blonde hair had turned into a ratty bird's nest. My green eyes seemed to be the only bright spot on a gray and spotted face – those eyes were alert and aware.

I wanted very badly to take a shower, but it felt so weird to be here. I quickly but thoroughly washed my face, then soaked my hair and combed it back with my hands. I washed my underwear and use it as a wet towel for my whole body. I enjoyed every second of this rapid (but luxurious) five minute act. Every day at home I would use gallons of hot water twice a day taking long showers, and I never really appreciated it. But this little cold panty sponge bath brought me joy in a dark place – amazing what a little bit of water will do.

I put my underwear back on, soaking wet. Even so, I felt much better. I felt clean. There was a towel hanging on the twisted heating pipe on the wall. It was a dirty, ratty towel, and I didn't want to touch it.

When I opened the door, my guard was standing in the same position as before, against the wall. He saw me, he nodded his head again, directing me back to the dark room where I had awakened. That was it, then – I had to go back to the room. I was to be a prisoner inside there.

What if I just tried to run away? I knew the way out. Would he shoot me? I had no idea where I was or what was going on. Maybe I would be released soon.

Anyway, the front door was locked. I knew that much without even touching it. And the man with the gun seemed belligerent towards me. If I tried to run and I got stuck at a locked door, he seemed like the type to tie me up and chain me to the radiator. I had seen exactly that type of thing happen in the movies. I didn't want to risk it happening to me. Better, now that I was awake, to take my time and think about what to do next.

We headed back toward the small and dark room.

We crossed through the bigger room again. It was much brighter than the one I was in. There was a red patterned rug on the wall and a red sofa against it. Also, there was an old small chest with a trifold mirror attached to it.

It took me just a few seconds to take in all the details of the room. The light and unpleasant color of the room's wallpaper gave me the impression that this flat was an example of the apartments that were brand new and released to the public in the 1970s or 1980s. Those were not the glory days of Soviet construction.

I remembered from my childhood that as soon as many Soviet families (including ours) got a brand new and free apartment, they began to make major repairs and improvements to it. Certainly, Soviet people appreciated any properties that they got from the government for free, and it was their choice to make a repair or do an improvement. Some people preferred not to bother – like the people who owned this apartment, for example.

Heavy dark drapes hung across the windows, tightened at the edges. Despite this, daylight penetrated into the room. Outside, the world was going on as usual. The sun was shining. Somewhere, people were laughing, and children were playing.

Back inside "my" dark, tiny room, feeling better from having bathed and used the bathroom, I experienced a growing confidence that I would soon be released. I refused to accept what was happening – it was definitely a misunderstanding, a terrible mistake. The strange country, the guard with the big gun, the abduction – it was not the story of my life! I was a free person, an ordinary student. I had never hurt anyone. I just lived my life, enjoying it.

What happened? Why am I here?

I was confused, certainly. But now that I had come to my senses, I was also positive that this situation would not last long, that everything would be clarified, and I would be going home soon.

I was still bothered by that window – no sunlight passed through it – it made everything in the room seem dark and hostile. Finally, I decided – I would take a look and see what was wrong with it. I walked right up to it and experienced a real shock. The window was like something from a scene in a horror movie.

The glass was painted black. The paint was solid, caked on in several layers. And it was not painted on the inside – only the outside was painted, or maybe between the panes. A person on the inside, locked in this room, could not scratch the paint off.

A cold shiver ran down my spine.

What kind of torture room is this? Who paints the windows with black paint?

Along the edges of the glass, the paint was less thick and therefore let some sunlight go through. I began to study it in more detail, trying to see what was outside. The window was surrounded by an old wooden frame that had been painted white long before, and now the paint was peeling off almost everywhere. I could see dark spots of wood underneath.

I attempted to look through the thinner layer of paint, and through the tiny gaps between the painted brush strokes. It was impossible. I could only recognize that the day was sunny, but I couldn't see anything outside the window – the slits were too small.

I needed to examine the window more closely. To do so, I would have to stand on the thick and wide windowsill. But I did not want to make any noise – I did not want the man to come in and restrain me. I didn't even want to attract his attention.

Everything in this room was foreign to me. I did not want to grow accustomed to it, or somehow be attached to it or associated with it. I did not want to settle down in it. I did not want to become comfortable there.

Instead, I just sat on the edge of the bed and waited. I had to be ready for the time when I would be rescued. Soon, this would all be over and I would be heading back home. My mom would cook something delicious, as usual. I would forgive Sergey for the argument, and life would be back on track. I would never forget this misunderstanding, of course, but I would remember these few days as a nightmare, something horrible, but temporary, and which passed quickly, like a childhood fever.

I had to remain strong – I would not cry, I would not beg for mercy – I would just wait a day, or maybe two. My mom and Sergey would find a way to pull me out of here. I just had to wait, be patient, be strong, and stay ready to escape.

Soon, the apartment filled with men's voices. Deep voices, laughing voices, menacing voices – all just on the other side of that locked door. It changed everything for me. I cringed with helpless fear and my heart pounded in my chest – adrenaline pumping through my body once again. Cautiously, I crept to the door and listened – I could not understand a single word they were saying. The voices brought back the painful memories of the darkness, the car, the monstrous people...

I was again in agonizing emotional pain. The foreign language of the men sounded like gibberish, a mad Babel – and I guessed that they were talking about me, saying the most terrifying things. I was not so much afraid that they come in and kill me instantly. That would not be the worst possibility. I was much more afraid to be tortured and abused. I was in panic. My heart was racing, I couldn't breathe. I nearly gasped for air. This couldn't be real! It wasn't happening. I would not believe in it.

I found myself back on the bed. I wrapped the robe around my body, hugged my knees and sat there trying to think. What should I do? I did not know.

Should I break the window to get out and run? I couldn't. I did not know what was going on behind it. I didn't even know what floor I was on. What if I broke the window and I was on the fifth floor? Even if it was the first floor, I didn't know where I was, or where I would run to.

The unknown was everywhere around me. And I was alone, all alone...

Time passed. Behind the gray door and the black window, life seemed to go on. I was completely cut off and isolated from the whole world.

Why?

On the other side of the door there were voices, and there was movement. The men were walking around, laughing out loud, and talking. A sudden sharp turn of the key in the lock made me cower in fear. I held my breath as the door opened. My room became lighter for just a few seconds. In the doorway, a man appeared and put something on the floor. He left quickly, locking the door again behind him. I didn't have time to ask him anything – but probably I would not have spoken anyway – I was in a complete stupor.

Curiosity and wonderful smell made me creep to the door to see what was on the floor. He left a plate, with a large piece of pita bread. I recognized it right away. It was delicious homemade eastern bread, which is baked in special ovens. At home, pita bread like that was sold in our local markets. Astrakhan is one of the most diverse cities in southern Russia. There are hundreds of different ethnic groups that inhabit it, with cultural influences ranging from Persian to Chinese.

Next to the bread, there was a glass milk bottle, filled with water or some other clear liquid. The bread had such a delightful smell, and my stomach cramped with hunger at the scent of it. I loved bread like that, even though I ate it very rarely.

As a child, before I was burdened by dieting to look good, I ate the bread by the ton, especially when it was hot – just out of the oven. I remember as a kid, my mother sent me to the store to buy a loaf of bread after school, almost every day. Sometimes I went together with friends from the block. We had to walk for twenty minutes to get to the store. The shop always had freshly baked bread in the evening. Each of us would buy one loaf of the still hot bread, and by the time we returned home, each of us would only have a quarter of it left. We would eat the hot and crisp delicious bread the whole walk back.

How great it was then – in carefree childhood!

Now, locked in the room, I was hungry, but was afraid to touch the food or drink the water. The water reminded me of how I had lost consciousness, and my dreary existence in a near-vegetable state. I suspected that the water or the bread might again be drugged or poisoned. I had to stay conscious and alert for when someone came to rescue me.

The day dragged on slowly.

The room grew darker, night pooling in the corners. On the other side of the door, the voices fell silent for a moment, then resumed again. Someone was talking loudly, very close to the door. My heart ached with fear at the sound of it. But nothing happened. I was forgotten in the damn room.

I was thirsty, but I would not touch water they had brought me. And I wanted to use the bathroom again.

My traitorous body had to shut down and hibernate! I did not want it to continue to demand the fulfillment of its physical needs. It wasn't fair. I wanted to stay in the room until someone came to rescue me. I didn't want to ask permission to go to the bathroom again. I'm not a prisoner! I felt humiliated, but my body would not cooperate with me – it wanted to drink, it wanted to eat, it had to go to the bathroom.

I needed to go again. I could hear the men behind the door, and I was terrified to leave the room. My mind invented horrible possibilities. I would be tortured to death. I would be dismembered, my organs cut from my body.

My heart nearly burst out of my chest, fear filling me inside. I was like a hunted animal, caught in a trap. Every sound – a creaking floorboard, a burst of laughter, something being dropped – made my body twitch and vibrate in terror.

I was paralyzed by fear of the unknown. I did not understand why I was there, why I was deprived of my own home, why I was deprived of my freedom. The helplessness and uncertainty burned me from the inside.

I knocked, and a moment later, the door was opened.

I was prepared to see the same tall man that was there in the morning. But a completely different person answered – a small man with an average build, a repulsively ugly man. He had closely-cropped dark blonde hair, and a beard. More precisely, his beard was just a thin hairline growing along the edge of his face. His eyes sparkled with cruelty. He looked like a serial killer, a very short one. Under his arm there was a holster hanging with a gun tucked inside.

"I need to go to the bathroom."

He grinned at me, and after letting the moment drag on several seconds, barely jerked his head toward the bathroom. His cruel eyes were like gun sights, and I felt them targeted on me. I tried not to look up, but I noticed a sleeping man on the red sofa. A machine gun lay by his side on the floor.

The light was on. The curtains were tightly drawn. Without raising my eyes, I slipped towards the bathroom. There were people in the kitchen – a few of them were talking and the door was ajar. Shorty followed very close behind me. For a second, I even thought he would follow me into the bathroom.

The toilet paper was still missing. I went out and asked to wash my hands. He grinned at me – there was something evil about his smile – and nodded toward the door. I went inside of the tiny bathroom. There was still no hot water – only cold.

I washed my hands with a dirty, disgusting piece of soap remnant that I found on the sink. Then I drank water right from the faucet – it tasted like rust. Again, I noticed that strange vessel with a narrow and long spout at the side – like those that I have seen on display in the Museum of East. It was almost like a teapot.

At that moment, from the depths of my memory, a piece of information emerged, a little fact that I had once read somewhere: Muslims do not use toilet paper when they go to the bathroom. They wash themselves with water. That's what the pitcher was for. It also explained why the toilet paper was missing.

I stared at the vessel. I would never ask these men about it. I would never say a word – it would be easier on my dignity to sneak a bottle of drinking water into the bathroom under my robe.

Something about the walk to the bathroom, and back to the room, under the supervision of the armed man, was hard for me. It was too humiliating to handle. I did not want to be a prisoner. I did not want everyone to know about my body habits. I wanted my freedom.

I do not know how it happened, but right before Shorty shut the door and locked it behind me again, I broke my silence. In fact, I almost screamed at him.

"Why am I here, you can answer me?"

Then:

"Can I speak to your boss?"

It was the wrong question to ask. I tried to say it politely, but instantly I realized my mistake. I should never have said a word. I did not believe he was the man in charge, and I had demonstrated this to him.

He froze, and then incinerated me with his eyes. The words flew from his mouth like the bullets:

"Shut your mouth and sit quietly if you don't want me to shoot your head off."

He said it in perfect Russian with a slight accent. He was so angry that suddenly I was shaking like a leaf in the wind. I did exactly as he ordered – I went inside and sat on the bed. The door closed and the key turned in the lock.

Dizzy from hunger, I looked down at the piece of delicious bread and did not know what to do. I needed food. I needed it to stay strong.

I ate it.

The bread was soft and delicious. I enjoyed every single crumb. It seemed like I had not eaten for ages.

The day faded, and the room sank into total darkness. I closed my eyes as I lay down in this strange bed, wrapped in a quilt blanket, thinking about tomorrow. What would it bring for me? Would I still be alive at the end of the day?

Sleep took me by surprise.

I slept the whole night, dreamless. I opened my eyes and the same dark confines of the room appeared. I was still in prison. The nightmare would never end! My throat was tight – it felt like I would choke from the terror and the sadness. Tears streamed down my face. I could not stand it anymore – to die would be better than to face another day in this room. I was lonely. I was miserable.

Why was I there? They hadn't explained anything.

What were they waiting for?

What was happening?

I waited, putting off the moment when I had to knock again and go to the bathroom under supervision. I did not have a toothbrush. I had no comb, no other clothing or underwear. My little black dress was a mockery now.

From the corner of my eye, I caught a movement in the dark window. Startled, I glanced that way, but it was my own reflection that I saw – I looked like a ghost in a long black cloak.

October 11ᵗʰ , 1994
Astrakhan, Russia

It was not like sleep at all. Every night, the woman fell into a trance, a spell, a stupor, where she went numb, then drifted off, carried away by her terror.

Somewhere between asleep and awake, in a fitful doze, a dream came to her – a blurry picture – in which it was impossible to see anything but the face of her daughter. The woman spotted her in the gray distance, framed by blond hair blown by the wind. The girl's face was obscured by the blowing hair – the woman could not make out her daughter's eyes.

She woke with a start, her breath caught in her throat.

The phone was ringing.

It was still very early in the morning – outside the window, there was not yet light in the sky. For the past week, she had lived as if in a coma. She did not remember how she went to work, and how she came back from there. She no longer lived in her former reality – instead, she lived in a nightmare world, a place where her only task was to hope for a call from the police.

Just yesterday, the police had accepted the case – they would investigate the disappearance of her daughter. Nobody knew where she was. The woman called every single friend of her daughter. Last she was seen at the restaurant across the alley with her boyfriend. He did not know where she was. Since then, the woman was always near the telephone. Yesterday at work, she had not left her desk for a moment. At home, she picked up the phone every five minutes and checked to see if it was still working. Her sole reason for being, the very center of her existence, was to wait for the detective to contact her.

Now, the sharp and alarming shriek of the telephone cut the dead silence of her apartment. She moved quickly through the shadows and went to it. With trembling hands, she picked up the receiver.

"Hello?"

A man's voice:

"Your daughter is with us in Chechnya. So far she is alive and well. We will exchange her for 300 million rubles. Get the money. I'm giving you two weeks. When I call back in two weeks, the money must be ready."

The woman nearly screamed it: "I don't have that much money! I'll sell everything I have and give it to you! Bring back my daughter! Please."

The phone was already dead – there was no sound except the jarring beep of a line that had been cut off. They had hung up before she even finished her sentence.

She froze. She could not breathe; she could not think – her head felt like a helium balloon on the end of a string. It would float up to the ceiling, then out the window, and far away over the city. She could not feel her legs. Everything around her seemed to warp and change shape - the inside of her home had become vague and formless – it had lost any sense of solidness or dimension. She leaned back against the wall and slid slowly to the floor.

CHAPTER THREE

October 1994
Grozny, Chechnya

I heard loud voices outside my room. There was something going on in the world just beyond my door.

Someone knocked on that door sharply – RAP, RAP – and without waiting for my permission or even a word from me, turned the key, opened the door, and abruptly entered the room. He looked around but there was nowhere to sit other than the bed where I was with my knees drawn up to my chin, and my arms wrapped around them. I was leaning back against the thin carpet, which covered the cool wall.

I was wrapped in the oversized thick robe. Ever since I'd had this long robe, it served as my only protection from the outside world. I would hide in it, wrapping myself up, so they could only see my head poking out the top. I did not have anything else in this ugly world – only this robe – a piece of worn out fabric. And I used it as a shield.

I knew it was dumb – the robe couldn't protect me from anything, not from bullets, not from the strong hands of the men if it came to that – but psychologically it helped. I felt safer wrapped inside it, like it could defend me from this armed mob of criminals.

The man sat on the floor and tucked his knees under as if he was kneeling to pray. He was stocky and short, with small jet black eyes, his movements were quick and sudden. His dark eyes drilled into mine. He looked sly and dangerous.

He had dark skin and the same closely-cropped haircut as the other men. Black hair framed a face with sharp features – his beard, trimmed to half a finger wide, connected with the hair at his temples. His nose was slightly long with a pointed tip. He reminded me of a fox – his eyes were not kind, but very, very tricky. He was dressed in jeans and a light camouflage military jacket, unbuttoned and draped over a dark t-shirt. He put both hands on his knees, then lifted a hand and stroked his beard quickly – everything he did was fast.

"What's your name?"

He spoke perfect Russian, but with a slight Chechen accent and some sort of strange whistling sound. The man had a speech impediment.

His small black eyes were hard, and I felt the hatred in those eyes. I squeezed my arms around my knees even tighter. The blood in my veins froze. I did not want to speak to this man. Very quietly, I pronounced my name.

"Lena."

He smiled a wicked smile, revealing small white teeth. It seemed that he was mocking me. It seemed that he would use those sharp teeth to eat me alive.

"Well Lena, are you scared?"

He looked at me like a wolf looking at its prey before ripping it into pieces. My heart stopped beating. I was not even sure if I was still alive at all.

"Don't be scared!" he said. "You are in Grozny, in Chechnya. Your mother will give us the money we want, and then you will go home. Nobody here will hurt you."

I stared at him. For a long moment, I could not understand what he was saying. Slowly, it dawned on me – they had abducted me for a ransom.

Oh my God.

He was still smiling, his eyes like lasers.

"Your mother has our money. When she returns it, you'll go home. If she doesn't return it, you'll go home in pieces."

I felt sick, and dizzy, like I would fall over sideways.

What kind of nonsense is this?

I was kidnapped, and they were demanding a ransom? And it was money my mother had taken? This couldn't be right.

Of course, I had heard about all the horrible kidnapping cases that had happened lately. I had watched movies about the children of rich people being kidnapped. Recently, I had seen horror stories about cases of abduction on the TV news.

It was terrible, even more so because there must be some mistake. Kidnapping only happened to people who were associated with organized crime, or to people who had a lot of money. Worse, in all the stories I had seen, none of the abductees were ever returned home alive.

I was the only child in my family. My mother always worked hard as an accountant, and she was well paid. We lived an abundant life – in the sense that we lacked nothing – but we were not even close to rich. My mom and my dad had divorced when I was in the 4th grade. I did not see my dad very often after that. He started another family and was busy with his new children.

My mother remarried, and we had a very happy family. I accepted my step dad and considered him my father. We traveled, had a lot of friends – we were the typical happy family. We may have lived a little better than average, but only because of my mom's and my dad's hard work and education. After my father died some time ago, my mom and I were left alone.

* * *

Russia in the 1990s was wracked by monumental, earth-shattering change. After the disintegration of the Soviet Union, a new history began. No part of life was unaffected by it. The decade was so turbulent, it became known as the Wild 90s.

For seventy years, the central government had controlled and watched over every aspect of life. In the late 1980s, this control started to weaken. Suddenly, in 1991, the government collapsed and absolute freedom came. The Soviet people gradually turned into a horde of alcoholics, drug addicts, thieves, rapists, murderers and maniacs. Until that time, all the vices and sins seemed to lurk behind the walls of a huge castle – imprisoned and held back by the all-powerful state. Once the state was gone, the ills of the world were set loose to run amok.

The criminal world took advantage of the USSR's collapse, and the country spiraled downward into lawlessness and corruption. Wherever they could, criminal businesses drove out legitimate activities. Businessmen competed by killing each other. It was a terrible time, accompanied by a deep recession in the economy and a surge in inflation.

In the 1990s, abductions for ransom became an established business practice. Bandit groups from many parts of the country engaged in it, especially Chechens. You could watch this play out nightly on the television news.

Now, I no longer needed to watch it on TV. I was part of it.

I sat in shock as I perceived the terrible news the man with the fox face dropped on me. How could it be? I was being held for ransom? I couldn't even imagine it. Even so, any hope that I had appeared here by accident collapsed. I was in captivity.

I sat huddled in a lump of fear and utter helplessness. I was in a panic – I wanted to cry. I wanted to beat my head against this gray alien wall. I did not want to believe this was happening. The most terrible thought, the worst-case scenario, which I was trying to erase from my head all these days, turned out to be the absolute reality. There was no misunderstanding – these people had kidnapped me on purpose. They even knew who I was. The terrible thought had now even gained flesh and blood in the form of the fox-faced man.

He had left the room as quickly as he entered it.

I was depressed and exhausted. Money… how much were they asking? Would my mom be able to find this amount? In any case, it didn't matter – I would not survive. The hostages were never returned…

I covered my face with my hands, fell onto the flat and cold pillow, and burst into tears. I was utterly helpless – I had no influence on what was happening, and the recognition of this seemed to tear my very soul apart. I lay there, with my knees tucked under me and my face down, wrapped in the huge robe. My tears flowed like a river, like a torrent, like the raging waters that come when the dam bursts, blocking me from breathing. I gasped for air. I felt so alone in this strange world, torn out of the water like a helpless fish, and thrown ashore to die.

Behind the door, the voices kept talking in their strange language. I could only guess at what they were saying – I just assumed and prepared for the worst. What could I do? I was not taught to survive in these conditions. I grew up surrounded by love and care, and in the comfort of my sweet and warm home.

I prayed for rescue.

I knew that the work had already begun – my mom and Sergey had gone to the police, and soon they would send a force necessary for my release. I should be ready for when they came.

Many times in the movies, I had seen how the commandos would use ropes to rappel down the sides of buildings, descending from the roof, smashing through the windows, saving the hostages and shooting or arresting the kidnappers. I decided that to avoid getting shot in the cross-fire, I could hide behind the bed, as long as I pushed it away from the wall a little bit in advance. Then, when the shooting stopped, I could quickly jump out the window into the waiting arms of the rescuers.

The window…

I had to explore the possibilities. In the dim light of the room, it was clearly visible what parts of the window were painted over less densely. To see through the gaps, I needed to get up onto the windowsill. I hoped that none of my abductors came into the room at that moment. I cautiously crept to the window and sat on the peeling window sill. It took me a few seconds to silently climb on it and start to explore the edges of the weird, dark glass.

Very quickly, my perfect plan for rescue, concocted entirely within my imagination, collapsed like a house of sand. Through a thin layer of black paint at the edge of the upper corner of the window, I could easily see the very recognizable landscape of a building courtyard. I had seen courtyards like this a thousand times, with another five story building just across the street.

In all of Russia, near the ground floor, the windows of buildings were grilled with iron bars to protect people's homes from being robbed. Each year, the criminal situation in Russia had worsened, so that now the windows were barred all the way up to the third floor. Instantly I saw that the apartment where I was held was on the first floor. No commandos were going to be able to burst through that window, and there was no sense coming down from the roof. Anyone who was trying to rescue me would have to stand outside the building, and try to cut the bars with an electric or gas powered saw – a loud, time-consuming, and utterly ridiculous method for breaking in. No would-be rescuers were going to come crashing in that way.

Through the paint and dust on the glass, I could see patches of trees with green and yellow leaves, spreading their branches under the autumn sun during what looked like a beautiful, and perhaps warm, Indian summer day.

Until that moment, I hadn't even realized how totally I was in prison. I wanted very badly to get out of there. I wanted freedom, fresh air, pure nature.

Why don't we appreciate the things that are given to us, when we have them? I had never enjoyed the frequent picnics in the countryside with my parents. I did not like to go pick mushrooms in the forest, or go fishing, or even to spend a night in our small boat in the Volga River delta. I thought of myself as an urbanite, a city person – I always preferred the comfort of my home over sleeping in a tent amid the inconvenient and uncomfortable outdoors.

How I would love to be back out there in the wild, right now! Would I ever experience it again? How much better it would be to be on the banks of the beautiful Volga River, or on our boat, rushing through the waves in the delta. I would give anything to be there, and not here.

The tiny room – my cell – was dark and depressing. Everything about it seemed heavy and threatening. I wanted – with every fiber of my being – to feel sunlight and breathe fresh air again.

***

A few days passed. I was trapped in a time warp.

Every day was Groundhog Day – it did not come to an end, but transitioned to the next, looking exactly like the previous one. Short dreamless nights turned into endless, pointless days, full of hope in the morning and sorrow by nightfall. I would prefer to never wake up at all, until the day of my salvation. At night, I could not fall asleep for a long time, listening to every rustle from outside the window and behind the door. I was ready, at any moment, to run from this room into the arms of my rescuers.

Most days, hope did not leave me. For a long time, I was absolutely certain that one dark night, the special police forces – a SWAT team, commandos – would storm into the building and save me. I was always ready for this moment. I would spend the whole day thinking about it, adrift in my imagination, developing possible plans for the rescue operation and how it might happen. I tried to picture it down to the smallest details, so that at the right time I would be ready to help the rescuers to save me.

It would not be easy – the terrorists were armed from head to toe. I imagined every single possible technical aspect of the operation, every likely scenario.

It was going to happen very soon. I could afford to be patient because this strange time was bound to be brief – it would not last much longer, certainly not too long to wait. I believed in this story and I lived by it. It was my religion.

But each succeeding morning I opened my eyes and I cried at my own helplessness, and at the unfairness of it all. I wanted to scream from the bottom of my lungs and go into hysterics, but I knew it would not help me. I kept struggling to remain silent, quiet and invisible. I was waiting for the rescue. I wished for this with all of my being.

Day passed into day, like the links of an endless chain, a chain that soon stretched into weeks. Nothing changed, and still I hoped for salvation.

Even though I never, not even for one second, wanted to get used to the idea that the present state of affairs was my destiny or my life, I still had to work out some way to organize my day. I had to have a schedule. Depression and loneliness helped me to some extent – I discovered that I had lost the taste for life, and I could lay down in bed for hours, staring at the ceiling without moving.

In the freedom of my past life, and being energetic by nature, I could not sit still. Now all of that power seeped out of me, like air from an old tire. My current life consisted entirely of humiliating trips to the bathroom and back, twice a day. This well worn path – back and forth – passing through the other room, offered me the only variety in my day, along with a glimpse of the outside world, the occasional sunlight coming through the windows covered with heavy curtains.

Then, back into the dark room, where I now lived and where time stopped. I tried to eat and drink as little as possible. I did not want to remind the men about myself. I knocked on the door only when it was absolutely necessary. I thought I would never get used to the bed, the food, and especially the bathroom. Everything in this place disgusted me. Because I knew I would leave forever very soon, I tried to minimize contact with the strangers' belongings and toilet articles.

There was never any hot water. After a few days without a normal shower, I learned how to "take a shower" using only the faucet and the sink. Since I knew that the door was guarded by an armed jailer, and the he could come in at any second, I took my sink showers very quickly. Using only ice cold water, I wiped my whole body with my lacy underwear, and the immediately put them back on to dry.

After two or three weeks, I knew there were always at least two armed men in the apartment. They all had weapons, mostly big machine guns. Besides the three guards, I would hear some other men come in – for periods of time, the space behind the door was filled with voices. Near the window in the bigger room, there was a large stack of the guns and ammunition. It looked like they were preparing for the war.

The room was furnished minimally – it did not seem to be owned by anyone. There were no extraneous things that might be the sign of the owner, except for a rolled mattress leaning against the wall. I began to get the impression that there was only one permanent resident there – me. The men who guarded me rotated and were replaced every once in a while.

Another place from which I could observe the outside world were the painted glass window in my room. I often climbed on the window sills and looked through the slits of the thin layers of paint. I did not notice a single person nearby. The streets, blurry as they were, seemed completely deserted. But even if I did see someone eventually, what could I do? Yell for help? That wouldn't work – the first ones to hear my scream would be the people behind the door. They would tape my mouth shut and tie me up. So I could not act recklessly. I had to come up with another plan.

* * *

The fox man came again a few days later. I sat on the bed leaning against the wall and remained silent, staring at a single point on the gray wallpaper. What could I do? The last remnants of my body's inner strength boiled inside of me, ready to explode in rage at my own helplessness. The man crouched on the end of the bed and spoke cheerfully, as if he was telling me not to be upset about a lost hair pin.

"Don't worry," he said. "Nobody will hurt you. In a couple of weeks, you'll go home."

I was infuriated by his tone. I wanted to wrap my hands around his throat and clench it in my grip just to shut him up.

The ruthless bastard – he didn't even seem aware that he and his gang had committed a crime against a human being, a crime that would leave a painful and permanent mark on the rest of my life, even if I went home right now.

Two weeks? I could barely last a few more minutes in this prison.

I didn't answer him. I was too choked up from outrage.

I was going to handle these days stoically, but to do so, I at least needed some hygiene items. I asked him for a toothbrush and a tube of toothpaste. I also mentioned something that was very much on my mind.

"The bathroom has no toilet paper," I said.

I did not want to complain. I just wanted to live my last few days with some dignity, some small amount of comfort, and without their anger escalating.

"Muslims don't use toilet paper," he said. "We use the jug of water."

I nodded. I already knew this answer and was ready for it. Okay. There wasn't going to be any toilet paper.

Beyond the lack of toilet paper, the trips to the bathroom themselves were a real torture for me – it was humiliating to knock on the door each time, and ask permission to answer my basic natural needs. I was not an animal, I was a human being. Asking to use the bathroom, then being shadowed down the hallway by an armed man – it tested my will and my sanity – and every day I had to pass this outrageous test.

I felt abandoned to survive on the island of a cannibal tribe. I did not know their language, and I couldn't predict what would happen to me next. They were from another world, they had their own customs, with which I was obliged to comply.

Why was this happening to me?

Privacy is a treasure – one I didn't even know I had until it was stolen from me. To live at gunpoint and under constant surveillance –

how long can a person endure such a life before she goes insane?

I didn't want to touch the food anymore. I tried to drink as little as possible to keep my forays to the bathroom at a minimum. I had to suffer for a few more days, and that was it. I forced myself to believe them when they said I would soon go home.

But the next few days turned into an eternity of waiting.

I waited and wished with all my heart, and wanted to believe that in a few days I would be home. A life of freedom looks completely different when you think about it while in captivity. The prisoner thinks, "When I'm free again, I'll never waste another moment of it."

When I made it home, I would embrace every second of my freedom. I would hug the people dearest to me – my mother and Sergey. I would never argue with them. I would always be kind and considerate of them. I was going to live my life differently.

My decision not to eat or drink anything soon had to change. I was losing strength. I could feel it ebbing from my body. I had been stashing the pita bread which they brought me every day in a drawer. I could not survive without fuel, so I took a big piece of the bread and ate it. Nothing had ever tasted so good.

* * *

And then came the black day. Or rather, the red day – I started my period. As if things weren't bad enough – treacherous natural processes of the body threatened my already precarious existence. What was I going to do? Knock on the door and ask if they have a few tampons to share? I had to find a way to deal with it myself – and I found it.

The sheet that covered the mattress on the bed was quite thick. Ripping it with my bare hands was not easy. I struggled for a while, my hands and wrists becoming sore from the effort, but finally the dense linen succumbed and I was able to pull apart two long strips. I made three rolls – the pads were bulky and uncomfortable – but still better than nothing. My thin lace panties could barely contain a huge chunk of the rolled fabric.

My body brought me untold difficulties – either hunger or thirst, or the need to go to the bathroom. Now I had another one. Why wouldn't my body go into hibernation, why wouldn't it switch to an extreme mode and abandon its natural needs, at least temporarily? Everything would be much easier.

At least now I knew why I was here. I was aware that at any moment everything could change. I could be traded for money, or I could be rescued by the police. Or, knowing that they couldn't get their money, the Chechens could cut my body into pieces and send the pieces home. Or they could just kill me – at the time of the money transfer or instead of it. Holding my breath, I would creep to the door and listen to them talking, trying to guess what they were saying by the manner of their speech or the tone of their voices. Everything was useless – their language had nothing in common with the Russian language, except for a few words that were international.

Time dragged by. I did not know what to do with myself. When I could no longer lay down, I would stand up and walk in circles in the tiny room. The people behind the wall lived a life of their own. I heard the door open sometimes, and someone would come into the apartment. Sometimes the voices I heard seemed far away – most likely they were in the kitchen. They would debate some point or laugh at some joke. Sometimes they were right in the next room, probably sitting on the couch, very close. It always seemed like they were about to enter my room and do something terrible to me. Despite the fact that I had felt a sense of fear every second, every minute, every hour, all day every day, and it accompanied me from the very first moments of the kidnapping, I couldn't adapt to it. It paralyzed me over and over again, as if for the very first time. It was impossible to control – I would never be able to get used to it.

Every human being feels a sense of fear throughout life. Fear – it's a mechanism that warns us of danger. A man is afraid of loneliness, and this makes him to search for a partner. The fear of hunger drives him to search for food. The fear of death – it binds us and compels us to act or obey.

I was not afraid of sudden death in these circumstances – the torture and the abuse frightened me much more. The fear for loved ones is the most intolerable fears of all, it corrodes your sole and destroys your well-being. I was terribly afraid for my mom, who must be suffering and could not know how to help me. I feared for her sanity.

As hard as I tried, I could not live the illusion of salvation and a happy return home. I did not believe them. I knew that kidnappers did not work cheap – they had demanded a great deal of money, which would never be found. It couldn't be found – my mother simply did not have it. I was afraid that they would cut off parts of my body, one at a time, and send them by mail as a warning. I would prefer a hundred instant deaths over torture.

I remembered the story that, I naively thought, was terrible enough. When I was in high school, we went by train on a school field trip to the so-called Golden Ring cities of Russia. In Suzdal, we visited the famous historical village, where all the details of the life of the previous century had been recreated. We tasted the water that had been carried from the well, we ate the bread baked in the special ovens – in general, we were trying to feel the lives of the boyars and the serfs.

Along with all sorts of interesting sights from the 1800s, our school travel group visited a nearby lake. There was the great centuries-old oak tree growing on the shore, spreading its huge, heavy branches just above the water. A rope swing with a wooden seat dangled from one of the heaviest branches. It was the same type of swing the boyars' children used in days of old. The swing was not a tourist attraction, but of course everybody wanted to take a ride over the lake on it.

The rope was long. When someone sat on the swing, another would pull it back and then with a hard push, launch it away from the shore, the person on the swing flying 20 feet out over the lake, before safely swinging back to dry land. Each of the students waited impatiently for their turn to experience this incredible flight over the huge pond of water. Finally, my turn came.

I clung with both hands to the rope and closed my eyes in excitement. One of my classmates drew back the seat and let it go. The feeling of free flight over the lake was indescribable! I felt weightless, like a bird. Especially the moment when I realized that something had gone wrong - the rope had broken and wasn't attached to the oak anymore. I flew over the pond - I'll never forget that feeling, that experience with the terror of the unknown – and plunged into the water still holding the rope and sitting on the swing.

Splash!

I opened my eyes.

The ceiling of the dismal room appeared above my head.

I was still here.

I remembered how I swam back to the shore and into the hands of the teachers who accompanied and supervised us. Needless to say the pond was not intended for diving. I was lucky enough not to come across the branches sticking out of the water and pierce my stomach. The teachers were scared – God forbid one of their students should get hurt on their watch. And I was scared, more so than they were.

I borrowed dry clothing from my friends – luckily some of them were wearing several layers. On the train, on the way back home, we were a gaggle of teenagers laughing and shouting about the incident.

* * *

Time passed in torment.

I was trapped, imprisoned. My personal space was reduced to a few square feet bounded by the four walls of a gloomy room. I was surrounded by people I did not choose, I could not understand, and who I nevertheless had to deal with. I was lonely for my mother and my boyfriend. The possibility of being subjected to violence at any moment slowly drove me insane. I was a bundle of nerves on the one hand, and on the other, I was indulging a fantasy that all of this would end in a few days.

I knew the room inside out.

The faded wallpaper told me that it hadn't always been dark in here. Some time ago, when the windows were not blacked out, these walls were getting enough sunlight to bleach out the color of the wallpaper. Near the windows, you could still see the original color – it was an ugly light brown, sort of yellowish. Perhaps it wasn't that bad under natural light. The dim light from the ceiling lamp made the color look worse.

I had decided to give the light a try after a few days. It hung lonely on an exposed wire and shone a dead color of light, and revealed a dismal room – the prison where I lived. The yellowish wallpaper, in some places stripped away, met brown painted moldings at the bottom. The floor was covered by an old gray carpet. The only furniture was the narrow bed and a bedside table near the window.

By far, the most interesting item in the whole room was an old Sharp cassette tape recorder. It even had an unlabeled cassette inside of it, the kind of tape you record songs onto yourself. It took me a while before I dared turn it on and check what was recorded on it. I fully expected to press the button and hear songs in Chechen language. I did not want to hear more – I had enough of Chechen language in my life.

I was so wrong. It was the Gipsy Kings!

The band played searing flamenco music. They were so popular in my hometown; you could hear them playing from every speaker. Their passionate love songs were listened to by everyone, despite the fact that nobody could speak or understand a word of Spanish. You were so swept away by the *feeling* of the songs; you didn't need to know what the words meant.

I listened to that tape over and over – very low in volume, bringing the speaker close to my ear. I would listen to one side, flip the tape, listen to the other side, flip it again and keep going. Late at night, in the total darkness, when the apartment was silent, the Gipsy Kings' beautiful and melodic songs played in my room, reminding me of my happy times while I cried quietly for hours.

* * *

As weeks passed, during my short outings to the bathroom I observed the environment and the people. In my own mental notebook, I classified the gang and assigned a nickname to every member I saw. There were about ten men who were often in the apartment. They rotated in and out. The man with the fox face – who I started to think of as Foxy – and the man I called Shorty, were the only ones who spoke to me. Maybe they were the only ones who could speak Russian.

The men were calm, and treated me well enough, as if they had been ordered not to damage the goods. All except for Shorty. He seemed like he could barely restrain himself from violence. He made mean-spirited comments about me, my mother and my boyfriend. He made comments about Russians in general. Sometimes he wrapped them all into one.

"You dumb bitch," he said, lingering at my door, a vicious smile on his ugly face. "Where is your boyfriend? He hasn't come to save you yet? Don't you know? He's off with another Russian slut by now – you're all the same anyway. And what about your mama? A dumb old sow, she does not care about you. She is happy that you don't bother her anymore. All you Russians... it makes me sick to think of you."

Sometimes he spoke in Chechen, causing wild laughter among the gangsters present in the apartment. I did not respond to anything he said. In my imagination, I saw him burning in hell.

I will go home soon.

I would sit silently all day, trying to delay my bathroom visits until the least amount of gunmen remained in the apartment.

Gradually, I lost track of the amount of time I was there. Besides the fear and the other emotional hardship, the shortage of simple things like water took its toll on me. I felt disgusting. I tried to keep myself clean as possible by bathing in the sink, but it was no good. I needed to take a shower.

Shorty's cruelty meant that I could not overcome my fear and speak seriously with him. I was sure that after learning about my desire to take a shower, he would scoff at this and not allow me to do it. He would take pleasure in my discomfort. He would destroy me with brutal jokes.

The other guards seemed too scary to talk to, or clearly did not speak Russian. The only candidate was Foxy. He appeared in the apartment mostly in the evenings.

My desire to get home was overwhelming. I missed my mom so much, and I missed my life. I dreamed that when I got home, I would take a long shower, enjoying every second under the warm and clean water. In the mornings, I would cuddle up in a plush towel afterward my shower and drink hot delicious coffee.

The ordinary things that we barely notice in the course of our daily hassles – I missed them so much. My hair was turning into straw, and my body had forgotten what soap was. The bathtub in this apartment was not suitable for using. The shower head was missing, and there was no shower curtain. No one had taken a shower here for years. But the bathtub itself still had a rusty faucet. I did not feel aversion anymore – I just wanted to bathe. I had to talk to someone. I could no longer do otherwise.

I waited for the evening. Standing at the door, I listened to the voices behind it. When at last I heard a whistling voice – the speech impediment of the Foxy man – I knocked. It was late now and the lonely dim bulb burned from the ceiling, dimly lighting my wretched home.

Foxy opened the door and looked at me with a question in his dark eyes.

"Tell me," he said.

"Listen, I realize that I'm a prisoner here, but I'm also a human being. I haven't taken a shower in weeks. Do you mind if I take a shower? I could use a bottle instead of the shower. All I need is a little bit more time in the bathroom, the towel, and shampoo."

I blurted it all very quickly and in one breath – I was afraid that he would not listen until the end and just slam the door in my face. After I spoke, there was a long moment of silence between us. I waited for his response.

"We'll see," he said finally, then shut the door in my face.

He did not say no – that was good.

The next day, as usual, one of the men brought me food. Along with the pita bread, I found a plastic bag that contained a clean towel and a half bottle of shampoo. I took this as an approval to use the bathtub. Foxy had taken pity on me. I waited impatiently all day for nighttime to arrive.

In the evening, he turned up himself. His head popped inside the door,

"You can take a shower right now."

I grabbed my simple belongings and went to the bathroom. Foxy escorted me. There were other people in the apartment. I didn't worry about them – my thoughts were filled with a rusty bathroom.

I held my breath as I opened the hot tap, hoping that this one time, something warm would flow from it instead of the icy cold stream I was used to. It was a privilege here. In all my days there so far, I had gotten lucky just a few times – taking my sink shower and washing my dress under a stream of warm water. None of this really surprised me. In Russia – a country with gigantic amounts of resources, a place with endless natural gas reserves – there were always problems with the hot water, and shutdowns of all supplies were not uncommon. It was akin to the Brazilians or the Colombians having a coffee shortage.

I unscrewed the faucet all the way. Apparently, the Hot Water God had mercy on me, because a lukewarm trickle flowed from the tap. That was more than enough for me. I had brought an empty bottle with me. The shower head might be missing, but the bottle was suitable for the task.

I stepped over the bath rim, inside the tub. I poured the entire bottle of warm water over my body. The feeling put me in a state of complete delight. I emptied the bottle over and over again, refilling it from the flowing tap each time. I could not stop. My pores hungrily absorbed the long-awaited moisture.

It takes so little to make a human being happy. A few weeks before, I couldn't have imagined living a day without taking a shower. The thought alone would make me depressed. Then again, prior to this ordeal, I had no idea what real depression was.

I spent an eternity in that rusty bathtub, pouring water and shampoo all over my body. No one disturbed me. I felt so refreshed – it brought me a sense of physiological cleansing. But nothing could cleanse the mess inside me. There was no balance, no peace. I was deprived of the most basic things in my life, but I was almost ready to accept that. I could live without them. But it was impossible to accept my lack of freedom; and to bear the separation from my loved ones was beyond my strength.

November 1994
Astrakhan, Russia

For the mother, life had ceased to have meaning.

After the first call, she had rushed to the police station with her story about the kidnappers and the ransom.

She was a bookkeeper by profession. She remembered that day, three months ago, perfectly, to the smallest detail. The company where she worked as a lead accountant received notification from the Central Bank to cash out a sum of money for a client. The amount was colossal, and she had a very bad feeling about it. Fraud was widespread since the collapse of the Soviet Union. She'd heard rumors of a new scam – the Fake Avizo Fraud, or "air money" fraud.

The scheme was simple – the Avizo was a bank transfer notice. The Central Bank would receive an Avizo declaring that in the next two weeks, they would be wired a certain amount of money from Chechnya or another far away region, to be transferred into the account of a particular company or enterprise. Although the money had not yet arrived, the banking system – still based on the old Soviet system – operated on trust. The accountant of the company receiving the funds in two weeks would have to cash out the money – and give it to the client – right away. But the reimbursement funds – supposedly traveling by the mail or by courier – would never come. Bank balances were only adjusted once a month or once a quarter, giving the crooks plenty of time to spend or hide the money.

On that day, three months ago, the woman had gone to the Central Bank with her suspicions. She decided not to cash out the unconfirmed amount in her local bank right away, but wait until the money arrived from Chechnya to the Central Bank. Of course, it didn't arrive.

Now, she was positive that her daughter had been taken because of the failed scam. The bandits hadn't gotten their money, and now they were demanding compensation for damages.

The investigator pretended not to believe the grief-stricken woman, and tried to get rid of her. The cops did not want to deal with the terrorists in their jurisdiction. It was too difficult for them, this new type of crime.

"Okay, ma'am. I promise you, we're working on it. If your daughter is missing, we'll find her."

The woman wanted to grab the cop by the shoulders and shake him. She wanted to shout in his face, if that's what it took to reach him. She wanted to fall to her knees on the dirty floor in front of him and pray to

God that this man understands her. Instead, she went home.

She was not looking for sympathy from relatives and friends. She needed professional help in the investigation of the kidnapping – help from people who knew what they were doing. She spent several days going from one office to another, trying to find the support of the authorities and get them to help her.

Russia has always been a bureaucratic meat-grinder that slowly but surely destroyed people's lives. People were fed into one end relatively whole and sane, and eventually they were spit out the other side, brainwashed, their bones and souls crushed, their spines ripped out and cast aside.

When you were happy, you always believed you were surrounded by a huge number of people who would stand up for you when needed. Once something terrible happened, the next moment the number of people around you was noticeably reduced. And, soon, you have no one and you are alone with your grief.

All you have to do is believe. Faith in God becomes the only thing that you can hope for in a moment of total and all-embracing despair. The more hopeless the situation – the stronger the faith becomes. In everyday chaotic vanity, we rarely think about the soul and are closed from dialogue with God, without distinguishing the warnings sent from above. In a period of loss and emotional pain, the mental organization becomes so vulnerable and hypersensitive, which makes it possible to acutely sense messages and signs of blessing. Faith is justified, and it is strengthened. Although the depth of God's providence is incomprehensible to the human mind - we gratefully receive the rewards sent to us for support. We find them where we expect them the least.

The woman was positive that the conscientious FSB officer, Vladimir, was sent to her from the above. She met him in an investigation arm of the state, what many people thought of as the secret police. Sincere and honest, the man understood the pain of a mother who had lost a child.
He procured and installed a surveillance device on her telephone and assisted her to get help from authorities. They finally launched an investigation to catch the kidnappers.

Vladimir took the woman to meet with an elder of the Chechen diaspora in the city – an old man from the one of the most respected clans in Chechnya, where family and clan ties are everything. The man listened to the woman's story and slowly nodded.

"It isn't right," he said. "They're young and foolish, but they will listen to me. I will go to Chechnya and meet with them. They will release the girl." The old man showed the confidence of someone who

49

enjoys high esteem in his community.

Taking advantage of his age and respect, he was sure that his admonitions would act on the bandits. He decided himself to negotiate with the kidnappers and rescue the girl from captivity.

CHAPTER FOUR

November 1994
Grozny, Chechnya

The war began November 26.

From my tiny prison, I could hear the far away echo of thunder-peal of shooting and the rattle of machine-gun fire. I did not know what it meant – I didn't even know there was going to be a war. I realized something else was happening, something mysterious, something dangerous.

I didn't have to wait long to find out what it was. Suddenly my captors, a criminal gang, had turned into a squad of militants. The apartment became loud with their rejoicing.

Just after dark, Shorty came to my door. He grinned at me, very pleased at my helplessness, and thrilled by something more.

"Russian pigs invaded Chechnya today," he announced. "They stormed Grozny, but their army was smashed by our men. Can you picture it? Hundreds of dead Russians, despicable cowards. They deserved to die. You were very unlucky to be born Russian, do you know that? Hardly a Chechen was killed."

It was impossible, too horrible to think about. *Hundreds dead?* I had become so isolated that the world outside my room had almost ceased to exist. My days were filled with loneliness and thoughts of my loved ones. I listened to music and cried quietly. I was hopeless, and useless, like a scrap of torn rag. All I wanted was to go home. Now this... news. The Russians had attacked Chechnya. Why would they do that? And they had been slaughtered. I could not picture what that would even look like. Somehow, it conjured an image of a medieval army on horseback, trying to storm a castle, arrows raining down from the walls. It sent a rude shiver through my body.

Could Shorty be lying about this? I studied him closely. No. He was very pleased, with his people, with himself for choosing to be born a noble Chechen – I couldn't tell. It seemed the violent death of hundreds of people was more than enough to make him happy. So it must be true – Russians had invaded and the Chechens had killed them. My face and body went numb as I absorbed the horror of it. Wars and battles had always seemed far away to me, abstract, something for other people to worry about. But I was here now, and somehow I was part of this, and it was part of me.

"See?" he said, smiling broadly as if his favorite football team had won an important match. "It is a very good day."

From that moment on, there was no longer quiet in the apartment. When I knocked on the door, I came face to face not with silent armed guards, but with joyful and self-righteous freedom fighters. All of a sudden, the apartment was full of weapons.

Shorty never let up – he tried to destroy my spirit whenever he saw me. He enjoyed humiliating the whole Russian nation and Christianity, trying to make me feel ashamed. I hurt so much inside but had to remain silent. How could I respond? I did not want to escalate the conflict with him – it couldn't bring me anything good. I could not fight against this horde of armed bandits. After all, I was their prisoner, and unarmed. Those first days of the war were a scary time. I was a peaceful person and far from politics, but every child in Russia knew where the Chechen hatred was coming from.

For two hundred years, Russia the powerful giant has dominated and controlled tiny Chechnya and its people. In the 1930s, Josef Stalin expelled the entire Chechen people from their lands and sent them to the gulag camps of Siberia. The ones who survived were allowed to return home in 1956, after Stalin's death.

When the Soviet Union collapsed, some Chechens decided they would be free from the Russians once and for all. A man named Dzhokar Dudayev became the Chechen leader, installed himself as President, and declared the independence of the Chechen Republic of Ichkeria, a country recognized by no one.

In Chechnya, Dudayev's propaganda work was built upon the hatred of Russia and Russians among the inhabitants. The people craved revenge for their losses under Stalin, projecting the pain from the past into today's world. Chechen men were shamed into fighting. Chechen propagandists poked their fingers from the TV screen, saying, "How long will you, a Chechen man, hide behind your mother's skirt? Pick up your gun and take revenge for the hardships of the past century." The insulted pride of Chechen men forced them to leave houses and they went to die for the financial interests of the leaders of Ichkeria.

But I was not the cause of the discord between nations. I was there for a different reason. I hated politics. I felt equally sorry for the Russian and the Chechen. Astrakhan was home to many cultures, and I grew up among them all, never separating my friends into the Russian ones and the not Russian ones.

There are enough bandits and crooks in any nation. So I just kept my silence. These men who held me were not political – they were criminals. I was almost grateful to them, because they treated me well. They gave me food and did not hurt me. It seemed like the most I could expect from them.

Maybe they were good people, who had set foot on the criminal path because of circumstances, or because they were brainwashed by the propagandists. Or maybe they were simple beasts, subordinated to an invisible someone who was more influential, and smarter, and who had not yet given the order to hurt me. I didn't know and I was afraid to look deeper. I was afraid to say anything in response to their celebrating. I was just afraid for my life and my well-being, especially because I would go home very soon. I did not want to make the situation any worse than it already was.

Shorty's favorite game was to humiliate me. He was a maniac.

"I saw more dead Russians today. Shot to pieces and begging for their lives, but they find no sympathy here. Such sniveling cowards, can you imagine? Why don't they send real men? Ah yes, I forgot. There are no real men in Russia."

The war had finally arrived. In fact, it had started weeks before – with little secret skirmishes - but no one had declared it yet. It had been a quiet little war, one which now would become much bigger and louder. Soon the entire world would hear of it and give a collective cry of horror.

Madness, the great statesmen would call it. *Sheer insanity. Butchery.*

But I knew nothing of war, this one or any other. The little I knew was that women didn't fight in wars. Lucky women stayed home while men marched off and fought and died in wars. Unlucky women were swept away by wars, and mowed under by them. They were chewed up by wars, and sometimes spit out. The politicians in Moscow wanted a war, you might even say they *needed* a war, but I also knew nothing of politics.

The war had come like a tsunami, or a hurricane, or a tornado, or some other natural force much larger than myself.

War is such a force, even though it is not natural. War is a giant, wanton, careless child. It breaks things, and then laughs in delight. And now I had become its plaything.

The hours of my captivity had evolved into days, the days into weeks, and now the weeks had become more than two months. Every day felt like an eternity. Something had gone wrong. I was still imprisoned, and hope was all I had to live by. But the war drained the hope from my body and my mind and my soul.

What hope could there be when outside the walls of my pathetic cell, people were dying by the hundreds? What hope could there be in the face of pointless cruelty? What chance of escape? Would I flee this place and run into the arms of the falling bombs and the spray of machine gun fire? No. The lights had gone out on my former sheltered life, and I descended, fully exposed, into the gathering darkness.

***

It all happened suddenly.

It was morning, and I heard a loud commotion outside the door – rapidly approaching footsteps and menacing male voices. Something dangerous was happening – this time I knew it for sure. My nerves were as taut as a ship's ropes. Adrenaline raced through my system. A thousand chilling thoughts pierced my brain – I was prepared for the worst.

The door opened and a short, stocky man appeared in the doorway. Foxy. From behind him, bright daylight burst into my room, streaming from the window in the larger room. I squinted in surprise as my gloomy room was instantly filled with light – after so much time in the shadows, the normal light of day nearly blinded me. For the first time, the curtains on the window behind him were thrown wide open. In my head the thought flashed: *they are going to execute me – I will be shot and killed.* They no longer needed to hide their location from a hostage who wouldn't tell anyone anything because she would soon be dead.

This day and all subsequent days, every time the door opened, I would be frozen in fear, expecting something terrible. Approaching footsteps or voices near the door would always bring the most horrible expectations. Emotionally I was ready to die. I was only hoping for salvation as I would hope for (but never expect) a miracle.

Foxy threw a plastic bag on the bed. He gestured at its contents.

"Put on this dress and shawl," he said, his voice whistling. "You're coming with us."

His voice was cruel. Something had happened and it made him

angry.

Everything inside me tightened again in a tangle of fear. Sometimes I still could not believe that all this was really happening, that it wasn't a nightmare. *What are they going to do?* An overwhelming sense of horror was my constant companion. I could never get used to this feeling, or accept the absurdity of this miserable situation.

In the bag, I found a long blue dress and a white square scarf with subtle brown patterns on it. The presence of the dress meant I had to part with the long pink robe, which I wore all the time over my black dress. I had to take off my imaginary shield, the thing that made me invisible, the only thing that protected me. I was used to the robe – I realized now that I *loved* the robe – and I did not want to part with it. But I did.

Now I was wearing a floor-length wool dress with long sleeves and a collar under the throat. It was dark blue. I took the little black dress – the one and only thing remaining from my past life – folded it and put it under the pillow, not knowing why. I did not know if I would ever return here again.

I covered my head with the scarf in the Russian manner, twisting it around my neck and linking the ends at the back, completely covering my blonde hair under the headdress. My hands and knees trembled. I was in an agony of terror. My life was over. Perhaps the same feelings are experienced by the prisoner sentenced to death. He does not know the exact time of his execution – he only knows that it is coming. There is no escape. He spends every day flinching at any rustle from behind the door. He does not live his life, he does not think, he simply exists and waits for the moment of execution, which could come at any second.

They came for me. The door opened and I went into the unknown. The big room and the corridor were filled with people – bearded men, all fully armed. Their faces were blank and their eyes were hard – killers, every one of them. The blood froze in my veins – there were too many men at once. I could not look at them. Speaking short guttural phrases to each other – it could have been dogs growling and barking – they led me out of the apartment.

Then we were outside in the cold air, moving fast. I couldn't see what was happening – the men surrounded me in a circle. All I could see was the light of day and the broad backs of the men in front of me. We sprinted, packed in a dense ring, from the building to the car – as if I was the head of state and these were the men assigned to take a bullet to protect me.

Someone pressed my neck down hard, forcing me to bow almost to the ground. The strong man's hand wrapped around my thin neck, his fingers like steel – he hurt me and shoved me into the back seat of a green military jeep. I prayed that someone was outside at this moment and called the police.

I lifted my head and looked at the street, as I awkwardly scrambled inside. There was not a single person around. The front yard of the building was completely deserted. I was right – I had been held on the first floor of an ordinary apartment complex that was built during the Khrushchev era. It was a residential district of five-story buildings - nothing special. But I suddenly felt how much I had been missing even this simple image. Trapped in my dark room, my mind had become a blank canvas.

The day was cold – early winter. There was a thin, nearly transparent layer of white snow on the ground. I was in the back seat between two armed men. They were talking in their hacking, barking, guttural language. I tried to listen to their words very carefully, but I couldn't understand a word. I did not know where they were taking me. I prayed for one thing: if they were going to kill me, please let it be instant death. I could not bear torture.

The jeep started rolling down the empty boulevard. I hadn't seen streets in what seemed like a long time. My world had recently acquired rather limited outlines – 12 feet by 12 feet.

Foxy was sitting on my left.

"Cover your eyes," he said in his hissing voice.

He handed me a piece of dark fabric. I wanted to see! But even that had to be taken from me. The endless feeling of fear had become an integral part of my existence. I did not want to cry in despair - in my heart I hoped that I was being taken to be exchanged.

Blindfolded, I pictured the landscapes that we were passing in my imagination. I could not enjoy it. Sandwiched on both sides, I felt the warm flesh of the two gangsters pressing against me. I knew I would never be able to cause them a sense of compassion. For them I was not a human, but only a means to an end, a way to make money.

After a time, Foxy's lisping voice ordered me to take off the bandage.

The blackness under the blindfold suddenly turned into gray – it was a gloomy, overcast day, gray skies, gray snowy streets – everything had the same bleak color. The car moved through the streets, into the center of the city, Grozny, the Chechen capital. The name of the city was all I could understand from the conversation of the gangsters. The further we went, the dirtier the road became.

Everywhere there was evidence of the recent fighting – bullet-scarred buildings, charred by fire, burned out Russian tanks and trucks thrown askew like broken toys. I was taking no sides in this war. I had my own war to fight – the war to survive, to stay hopeful, to stay alive... to be saved.

Outside the window, the picture became even more terrible. The trees were bare, and the new snow was mixed with mud and blood, white and brown mixed together, with jarring smears of bright red. Here the buildings were destroyed, crushed and smashed as if by an army of giants – we were right in downtown Grozny. I stared in shock at the wreckage – I had never seen a war up close.

The car stopped at a plaza in the center of the city. They parked near a large tree with massive naked branches spreading out to the sides. I looked around in a stupor, and soon I noticed something lodged between the thick branches. It wasn't one something – there were several of them. At every crook of the bald tree, one of these things had been carefully placed. I stared and stared at them, trying to make out what they were.

Foxy spoke, the intensity of his voice startling me. "That's what will be left of all the Russians who come to our country."

They were human heads.

Cut off heads of Russian soldiers, plastered with mud and blood, decorated the tree like Christmas bulbs. They were probably very young – they had been boys just recently – certainly so young that they couldn't even hold their heavy guns right. They had been called up for military service only yesterday, and now they had to remain here forever. Their mothers must be...

I couldn't think. I couldn't face it. A wave of dizziness and nausea passed through me. *How is this possible?*

Around me in the car, the gangsters prattled among themselves in their unknowable language, their voices excited and cheerful. They were happy. No, they were jubilant. This atrocity, this disgrace... for them, it was a victory to be celebrated. They had won the first battle, but not the war. I stared straight ahead, my face numb from the horror.

The car lurched into motion again. I expected that I too would be beheaded, and soon, so I prayed quietly and thought about my mother. It only took another ten minutes to reach our next destination. We came to a stop.

"Listen to me," Foxy said, his lisping voice right in my ear. His mouth was so close that I could feel his breath. Then we were face to face. My own breath caught in my throat. His dark eyes bored into mine. His teeth seemed sharp and dangerous. I was so deadened by fear, his words did not reach my brain right away, though he spoke simply and with barely an accent. He spoke seriously, his words angry and abrupt, pronouncing each phrase in a clipped and threatening manner. I looked into his close-set eyes, trying to find some humanity in him.

"We're going to get out of the car, and you're going to talk to your mother over the phone."

I gasped. *I'll be talking to my mom!*

"Tell her she has to find the money. The full amount. Tell her that you're alive and you're doing well. So far. Tell her that if she gets the money, you will go home unharmed. If not, you'll go home in pieces. In two weeks I will cut off your first finger and send it to her by mail. Tell her that. But behave yourself. If you try to scream, no one will help you, and it will only make things worse. I'll shoot you in the arm or the leg, and you'll sit chained to the radiator for the rest of your time here."

Foxy's words shocked me like a bolt of lightning from a blue sky. I was not a hero; I was not a special agent trained by the military. I was an ordinary Russian girl. I had never encountered violence in any form before, but in the course of twenty minutes I had seen dead boys with their heads cut off, and now a man was telling me he would cut me into pieces, or maybe shoot me and chain me to a radiator. I had no idea how to react to the things he was saying – they simply terrified me.

But besides the overwhelming fear, another feeling absorbed me even more. I would hear my mama's voice! I missed her so much. It was excruciating. I knew how anguished she must be over my kidnapping, but I had no way to comfort her. She probably didn't know if I was even still alive.

The jeep was stopped in front of the main post office.

For a while we stayed inside the car, as if the men were waiting for a command. Suddenly, everything was set in motion, all four car doors opened at the same time, and all the kidnappers hurried to get out. They didn't have to push me out of the car - I could not wait to hear my mom's voice. I jumped out almost instantly, along with Foxy and the three others. There were another three men outside. I was once again pressed inside a dense circle, surrounded by the men. I couldn't see, but I also didn't care. I couldn't wait to get into the building. A few quick steps and we were on the tiled floor in the building's cool lobby. It was a standard Russian post office. One side of a large hall was lined with telephone booths. On the opposite side, there was the telegram office. A few people milled around, sending letters, making calls – who knew? They didn't seem to notice us at all.

Our tight circle moved quickly down the hall, feet stumbling to keep up, my heart torn by impatience. At the end of the hall a door opened, and I was pushed into a tiny phone booth. Everything happened at lightning speed. Someone gave me the phone receiver already warmed by someone else's hands. I pressed it against my ear.

"Mama?"

I could no longer hold back the tears. They ran down my face. I was dying inside - how badly I wanted to dissolve from here and appear at home! I couldn't stand it anymore. Anguish and pain and fear tore me to pieces. On the other end of the phone line I heard the breath of the most wonderful and lovely person - my favorite person in the world. I could feel her there. I felt her struggling not to weep too, and not fall into despair. I knew that she did not want to show me how bad and hopeless everything was.

"Sweetheart," she said, and paused, and I heard how she swallowed a lump of tears in silence. She did not want me to hear it. Her voice entered me, and tore me up inside. I wanted to die and not feel this unbearable pain any longer. My mom's voice sounded dry and cracked after spilling so many tears.

But she tried to instill hope in me.

"Sweetheart, are you ok? Are you hurt? I'm going to get you out. Everything will be fine, and we will meet again very soon."

"Mama, I'm okay. They just want money."

I held the phone and I did not want to let it go - I wanted to stay here and listen to her voice forever. I was supposed to tell her that they planned to send me in parts, and in two weeks they would cut my finger off. But I wouldn't do it. It would be better to be killed right now, right here, rather than cause her any more pain.

"Sweetie, everything will be okay." She spoke to me in a comforting tone, as in the days when I was a child. She talked to me, her voice washing over me, the words not as important as the sound of her voice. Her talking alone made me feel better, just like in my childhood.

Someone started to pull the phone away from me. I grabbed it with both hands, fighting him. I did not want to leave the booth.

"I love you, Mom!" I shouted.

I heard her screaming. "I love you, Lena! I love you!" At the end, her voice turned to sobs.

Someone dragged me from the booth. Stone hands twisted my arms behind my back, snatching the phone away. I couldn't see – tears filled my eyes.

They raced me back through the post office, pushing me, dragging me. In seconds, I was inside the car. I covered my face with both hands, bent over, and hid my face on my lap, sobbing silently. I didn't want to look at these men. I hated them with all my heart and wished them only death.

December 12, 1994
Astrakhan, Russia

For the woman, each new day was just like all the previous –
overflowing with sorrow and grief. The woman avoided people, staying
at home all the time, dedicating herself to waiting for the abductors to
call. She did not go to work, fearing to miss a phone call. Would they
ever call again?

The elder had met with the kidnappers, but the operation had failed
completely. The angry terrorists did not heed the exhortations of the
elder, and promised revenge on the prisoner if their demands were not
met.

For the woman, hope, which had appeared for a moment, now
collapsed. There was no hope at all anymore. All that was left was pain,
as if part of her very self had been torn away, and terror for her only
child. She did not know how to weather the grief. She no longer spoke.
She no longer listened. She no longer thought. She caved into herself.
Guilt and powerlessness led her into a downward spiral, deep into
depression, and then past it, down into something like quiet insanity.

One day, the telephone rang.

With aching heart, she picked it up - the receiver weighed a
thousand pounds.

A man's voice was there:

"You will speak with your daughter in a minute."

The woman froze, as if shocked. It was almost impossible to
believe that she was going to hear that sweet voice...

"Mama!"

How much she loved and how much she missed her! She was ready
to endure any pain, any physical torture, if only it would bring her
daughter home.

"Sweetheart..." she began. The lump in her throat made it hard to
speak. "Sweetheart, are you okay? Are you in pain? I'm going to get
you out. Everything will be fine. We will meet very soon. My love, do
not lose hope. We should be strong. I'm doing everything to bring you
home very soon. We just need more time."

She didn't believe her own words. Only moments before, she had
been abject, with no hope for the future at all. She still had none. Now
she was telling her daughter not to give up because soon she would be
home. She was lying, not just to the girl, but to herself as well. She told
a lie because the truth was too hard to face, and because maybe her
daughter would believe the lie. She also told it because it was just

possible that she herself might come to believe it.

"I love you! I love you!" they shouted at the same time.

At the other end, a rough man's voice replaced the sound of her daughter.

"You have three more weeks to get the money. This is your last chance. You've made me angry. After three weeks, you will get her finger in mail."

He hung up.

The woman sobbed, wracked with the searing pain of loss. The floor seemed to fall away under her feet, along with the last of her strength. She cried out and dropped to her knees, shivering uncontrollably.

December 1994
Chechnya

My mother's voice froze in my mind. I could still hear her words. With every single cell of my body I could feel her emotional pain and how much she was suffering. I knew how difficult it was for her to restrain her tears, and show me some way to remain strong in the face of a hopeless situation. It was as if I was trapped at the bottom of a black hole in the earth, an abyss, and she was trying to throw me down a long rope. But deep inside, I knew her efforts were futile. The rope would never reach me, and it wouldn't help me climb out anyway.

My heart was broken. My mother was the most important person to me in the world – no one else even mattered. We had been fed into the meat grinder of the criminal-political system, we were torn to shreds, and we were helpless to do anything.

I sat silently shaking from heavy sobs, but the tears did not stop – a river flowed down my face. My eyes hurt from crying so much. The Chechen madmen drove me back through the deserted streets to the gray and cold room. I fell into the bed exhausted and spent – totally drained, both physically and mentally. I had to wait.

"I have to be strong," I told myself. "This will not last long – I will be saved. It will all soon be over." I tried to believe it – not because I thought it was true, but just because it was what my mother had told me.

After a while, I had no more tears to cry, and lying in bed, I recalled the painful details of the day. I had been so overwhelmed by my own feelings during the trip, that I didn't pay attention to what was happening around me. Now, in the darkness, I tried to remember everything to the smallest detail. I wondered how it was possible that all the abductors were carrying huge automatic rifles, out in the open. None of them had tried to hide their weapons from the random people around them. Was it the war? Was it Chechen society itself – the endless permissiveness for the crooks, abductors and gangsters?

With the onset of winter, behind the black window, the bright days became shorter, but despite that they did not seem to pass any more quickly. I was no longer able to navigate time – all I could do was wait. The minutes came to be hours, the days an endless perpetuity. Once there were green bushes outside the window, but now they were completely naked, and the weak sun shone on a deserted courtyard. Through the thin slits between the black paint, it was now almost impossible to see. Everything merged into a sinister gray mass. Time had stopped. There was no one out there at all.

The people had left their homes long before the first assault on Grozny. The Russian government apparently thought they could take over the country with a handful of young soldiers, back in November. That never happened. On December 31st, the real war, the serious and bloody war, began. Hundreds of Russian armored vehicles, heavy artillery and aircraft entered Chechnya.

I knew that the war had started. Shorty told me.

"Your Russian bitch bastards wash in their own blood. We will cut off the head of each, and send them by mail to their mothers."

I was slowly going insane.

The monotony of my existence was suppressing my mind and personality. Every morning, I assured myself that the new day would bring me salvation – thinking that was the only way I could cope. But by nightfall, I was positive that I would not survive the next day, and I would fall into despair. My life seemed senseless and dead-end. One of the worst things in isolation and captivity is that emotions are experienced much more sharply, at their extreme. Pain turns into agony, and fear into paranoia, the helplessness into despair.

Shorty continued to humiliate me.

My life was difficult enough, and now he was turning it into an everyday torture. He would not leave me alone. He would drop into the apartment, open the door to my room, and stand in the doorway, playing with his gun in front of my face.

"I executed five Russian pigs today. Weaklings who surrendered instead of fighting to the death like men. They died anyway, sniveling cowards, on their knees. BANG! BANG! BANG! BANG!"

He paused, letting it sink it.

"And one last, crying as I put the gun to his head. BANG!"

I became paralyzed with fear - almost as if my body had turned to stone – whenever he appeared, but even so, I could barely hold my tongue. The witnesses of his mockery watched it, amused. When he got tired, he left, and I felt an indescribable joy. I dreamed that he would die in the war.

He was my worst enemy.

I could not wait for nightfall, when the apartment was quieter. The militants dispersed to fight or to spend a night at their own homes, except for a couple of guards who were always there. The night was mine - in peace and tranquility. I played that single Gipsy Kings cassette in the tape recorder, holding the speaker close to my ear, the volume low, so no one could hear it behind the door. I listened to the delightful guitar playing and passionate singing, memories flooding back, and I would sit behind the closed door, isolated from the whole world, and dissolve into a puddle of grief. I mourned my miserable life, recalling the carefree and happy days of my childhood and adolescence.

CHAPTER FIVE

January 1995
Chechnya

I heard Shorty's voice right at the door.

The hatred in me started boiling. I was full of poison – they had poisoned me the first night, and it had never left my body. It pumped in my veins now, a diseased revulsion for all of these people, and especially him. I hated him with all my soul and with all the blackness inside my heart. I wanted him to die. No. To simply die would be too easy for him, and too sweet. I wanted him to go out slowly, in pain, and in terror, and in humiliation, like the humiliations he delivered to hapless Russian teenagers, conscripts, which he so enjoyed describing in minute detail.

I sat quietly on the bed, afraid to move. The lamp shone dimly.

"Don't come in," I said silently, in my mind. "Please don't come in here."

He read my thoughts and hurried to torment me. The door opened. He was very short, the caricature of a capering gnome from childhood nightmares. His beard was uneven, as if the pockmarked skin of his face was contaminated ground, and the hair was so sick it could not bring itself to grow. It did not have the strength to escape him and breathe the fresh air.

He casually held a long machine gun with one hand. It was strapped over his shoulder, a monstrous thing, and he was clearly proud of it. It hung down with the barrel almost touching the floor, because he was so small. He was like a toddler, precociously playing with his big brother's toy. But he saw himself differently. He stood in the doorway grinning, the master thespian, warming up to play his role. The audience in the other room had yearned all day for one of his famous performances.

"Well, shall I tell you a story about your Russians?" he said. "We have a few of cowards in captivity right now – in the pit. We haven't decided what to do with them yet. Today we had some fun. I cut the tongue out of one of them, because he couldn't speak Chechen. Tomorrow I'll cut his ears off, and bring them to you."

With pounding heart, I was there just motionless, staring at the wall in silence, shaking with hatred. He was angry.

"Get up when I talk to you," he ordered.

I wanted to die right there. I was overwhelmed with fear, hatred and despair. I was ready to explode.

"Get on your feet!"

I slowly began to crawl out of bed and stood in front of him at my full height. I was a little taller than him. Our eyes met and suddenly I burst out:

"Do you want to know *who* the real coward is? It's you!"

The whole apartment was deathly quiet. At that moment, I could no longer think. Everything dropped away – all I could see was his ugly and distorted face. He was like the villain in a medieval fairy tale, a small gnarled monster that hides under a bridge and eats passing children. I didn't care what he did. He could kill me, but nothing he might do mattered to me anymore. I could no longer hold it in: I started screaming at him, all of my pent up hatred and terror spewing out, the accumulated poison of months of helplessness in every single word. Shorty stopped and stared at me in a stupor.

"Only a true coward could humiliate an unarmed person, especially a woman, holding a machine gun in your hands! I don't have anything! Give me your gun, and then we'll see who the real coward is, and whose ears I can bring to *you!*"

I spit the words at him. I had no way to frighten him, except with my own voice. My fists clenched painfully. The burst of emotions coming to the surface set the skin of my face on fire – I could feel myself burning alive.

His eyes were bloodshot, his face twisted in anger. He moved fast, almost leaping close to me, like a dancer. Then he punched me in the stomach. Instantly, I doubled over in pain. I could not breathe and fell back into the bed, hardly trying to inhale air. Someone else came into the room and started speaking to Shorty in a fierce whisper. A few seconds later, Shorty left.

I lay bent over, clutching my stomach with both hands, barely breathing. I was sure my lungs were collapsing. I wanted to puke, and I wished I would die. The newcomer quietly sat down on the bed and patted me gently on my twisted back. Then he went out.

I could not straighten up, and lay there all night, crying from the loneliness and embarrassment, my face buried in a pillow wet with tears.

Eventually the morning came and with it, a sense of something new and miserable. I was sure that the worst part of my life was about to begin. Shorty was going to make my life the ultimate hell.

I was no longer able to resist the inevitable. If I could not be exchanged for money or Chechen prisoners, I was done. If not physically, then certainly emotionally – my mind would not last.

January 6th, 1995
Astrakhan, Russia

The woman drew the heavy curtains in every room, turned off the lights, and in the impenetrable darkness, she lit the candles. As always, once a year, at Christmas, she began her ritual of divination.

With trembling hands, she crumpled a piece of paper into a ball, put it on a tray and lit it. The dry paper caught immediately. Dancing flames threw shadows on the wall. She stared at the fire thinking about her daughter.

Are you alive? Where are you? Will I ever see you again?

The paper soon burned down. She stared without a single blink, scanning the outlines of the burnt paper in the light of the candles, hoping to see the future.

She eagerly peered into the shadows: she saw the side of the mountain, and a barely discernible human figure. Her heart pounded. She began to look closely to the details of the figure. It was a girl, hair blowing in the wind. The woman could not understand whether the fragile female figure was walking or was frozen – left forever, on the slope of a high mountain.

The woman breathed heavily. She sat down on a stool and closed eyes. What if her imagination was playing tricks? Her head was spinning, temples throbbing.

She was afraid to open her eyes and see the motionless, trapped forever between the mountains, female figure on the wall, in the dancing light of the candles. It would break her heart and kill the woman's spirit and faith. She could not let this happen. The woman was excited and exhausted.

She opened her eyes firmly and rapidly blew out the candles, without looking at the shadows. Groping in the dark, she went into the bedroom. It was long after the midnight. She collapsed on the bed and lost herself in disturbing dreams.

January 1995
Grozny, Chechnya

There was movement behind the door. I heard voices, and the sound of a visitor. Someone was going to come in. I knew all the sounds by now. Each approaching step became louder and louder, like an alarm right in my ear. I imagined how the evil Shorty would come in and simply shoot me. I was hoping for it. I no longer wanted to endure beatings and tolerate bullying. Someone touched the door handle, turned the key twice and I squinted, holding my breath...

The door opened and I saw the fox face.

In the weak light of the room he came closer. I could see he was holding a large glass jar filled with canned fruits in liquid, the kind that are made for winter time. I watched him carefully, with suspicion. He put the jar on the floor and sat on the edge of the bed. I huddled in the corner and did not know how to react.

He put both hands to his beard and smoothed it.

"I brought some peaches for you."

There was a long pause, a moment of silence between us, and his sharp black eyes pierced my soul.

"I'm Aslan," he said with a whistle.

I stared at him.

"Don't be afraid. Mirza won't touch you. He is just a little pissed off. His brother was recently killed."

I remained silent. I just listened. I had no desire to talk to him, and no plans to believe what he said.

He grinned weakedly.

"Are you sure you're Russian? You have spirit. I respect the power of the spirit."

He left. Shorty Mirza did not appear all day.

Foxy had a real name now – Aslan. He showed up again the next day. His little black eyes always had a penetrating look, just as his face always had a smile.

His smile did not cause me to smile back, but only to shrink away in fear. He kept smoothing his beard before saying something, all the while staring straight inside of me. He was short and muscular, with jet-black eyes and hair – a true son of the Chechen mountains. There was some kind of primordial power and inner strength in him.

And all of a sudden he began to take care of me. He didn't make a show of it – perhaps it was not even noticeable to the others. I felt it.

After the incident with Shorty, something had changed. I was sure: I'd been there more than three months, in almost complete isolation, under constant supervision, and I had barely said a few words during all that time. I was forlorn. I did not have anybody who would show me the smallest sign of care. Now I started to feel it.

A few days later he came to me in the evening with a big jar of the home canned cherries. He slipped into the room almost like a ghost, without making a sound. He sat on the opposite side of the bed, and as the considerate host inquires of the guest, asked:

"Do you need anything?"

"Yes, I do. Freedom. Let me go."

His grin stretched into a wide smile and he laughed quietly, almost silently.

"I can't let you go. Eat some cherries."

To my surprise, I had a companion now. Almost every night, I saw Aslan. He was a guard, or just present in the apartment, in the evenings. He came into my room, sat on the bed with one leg tucked under him, and we talked. I was glad that at least I could talk to someone now. Time passed a little faster. We talked about war and politics. He described how the dishonorable Russian troops conducted the war, and how courageously the Chechen Vaynakh fought.

The more he mentioned this word, the clearer its meaning became to me. He called Vaynakh his brothers in spirit and faith. Their honored traits were courage and honor, and commitment to the Chechen nation. Their highest value was freedom.

How ironic that their lofty ideal was the very thing they deprived me of.

The thought of escape never left me.

Because of the war, the gang grew, along with the pile of weapons that I observed on the way to the bathroom and back. The gangsters and the weapons lived symbiotically, feeding each other, giving each other health and life. As one group multiplied, the other did, too. If the war was a heavy spring rain, then gangsters and guns were the mushrooms sprouting in the forest.

Now there were a lot more of both.

In one of the escape plans I drew up in my mind, I considered stealing a weapon, but the opportunity never came - I could not even come close. I thought if I had a gun, I would be ready to shoot anyone on my path. In my imagination, I planned a massacre of everyone in the apartment, and then I would escape. The only thing missing to complete my plan was a gun. I still kept hoping that one day, the police or the troops would find me and save. Russian troops were so close, after all. I even imagined Sergey, armed to the teeth, breaking into the apartment and ruthlessly killing everyone and liberating me.

I thought about my mom, and could not hold back the sobs. *How was she coping with this? Was she even alive?*

I was ready to leave this place at any moment. Leave forever and never come back.

One day, my thoughts materialized. In the evening, the space behind the wall was filled with an unusually large number of voices – it did not cease until late at night. I couldn't wait until all the sounds were silenced, to knock on the door asking to go out of the room. Eventually, the place quieted down – most of them had left.

I went into the bathroom and instantly spotted the gun. It was resting on the floor – a black pistol with a brown handle. I had been dreaming about it for so long, I almost couldn't believe it was really there – I had been given a gift. With shaking hands, I picked it up, hid it under my dress, and brought it with me into my room. It was not big, but it was heavy. Maybe it was fully loaded.

I was not afraid of weapons – I've always loved them. All of the children received basic military training at school, and it was there that I discovered my passion for weapons. The lessons were my favorite ones in school.

I was an excellent shot – in school competitions, I was one of the best with a rifle. I could disassemble and reassemble an AK-47 in a few seconds. But I didn't know anything about pistols. Was it loaded? Would it shoot when I pulled the trigger? How many bullets did it have?

I carefully held it in my hand – a small device with such great power. I could take away the lives of the men outside that door. As many lives as the gun had bullets. Having the gun gave me strength. If I could shoot without a miss, and without hesitation, I would be able to escape. In my heart, I had always wished my captors were dead.

But could I kill?

I replayed the plan in my head over and over. It seemed so real. I could knock on the door and kill the person who opened it, right from the distance of my arm's length.

Doubts plagued me.

It was against my instincts – to kill another person. It was against human biology itself. But no, wasn't violence part of human nature, especially in a situation like mine?

I was alone, and there might be more than two of them. They would kill me before I could kill them. Then they would kill my mother and all my family and relatives. I was paralyzed by fear – I could not foresee how events would play out.

I wanted to save my life by taking away other people's lives. I had planned the murder and escape in my imagination, relying on the movies I had watched and books that I had read. But my reality was far from a movie. It would be much easier to commit an unplanned, accidental murder. Having the plan to murder someone, and then sticking to the plan – it was impossible for me.

I could not change myself. I could not kill.

To continue living in captivity was not an option for me – it was beyond my fading strength. Every day, every hour, every minute of time that dripped by, I could feel myself fading – the life force that had long nourished me was fading, drying up, growing brittle and weak. It could crumble to dust and be blown away by a stiff breeze. With a gun in hand, though, I could put an abrupt end to my long downward spiral. I could decide my own fate, if no one else's. All I needed to do was pull the trigger. One bullet – and I could, once and for all, end my suffering.

I squeezed the pistol grip, and pulled the trigger…

BANG!

I fired a shot into the wall and threw the gun on the floor.

The sound was loud. It started a commotion in the apartment. Someone ran to the door and opened it quickly. I recognized the silhouette of Aslan, followed by two other men. There was a complete silence for a few seconds. I was nailed to the edge of the bed.

"I could have killed you all, but I didn't. Go and live."

I could not find anything else to say. My hands were shaking, I was trembling like a leaf in overwhelming unpleasant excitement.

Aslan picked up the gun and stared at me in the dim light for a long time – his foxy animal grin was gone. Then he left the room.

I cried all night, hating my weakness and regretting my failed chance. Maybe it was my last and only chance for salvation.

Time passed – there was no salvation.

My senseless existence was hard to call a life. The days passed. The bleak light in the room was different in the morning from the afternoon, so I could tell that time was lapsing. Then the long night would come, followed again by the day. It seemed that a hundred hours could march by, slowly, like mourners at a funeral, and besides the idea of escape and the image of my mother's face, I might not have a single cogent thought. Each day was an eternity. I was in deep space now, where time no longer existed. These men had broken me away from the world. They had broken me from my friends and family, and even from myself. I couldn't imagine a person more fractured and splintered than I was.

The military action changed the gang's plans. The war was coming – the front kept moving closer to the place where I was kept. Now I could understand why the area around the apartment building was deserted. The men had left their homes and joined the rebel forces. Before the war started, the women and the young children had moved to the homes of relatives in the remote villages. I was almost at the epicenter of the fighting. Terrible echoes of war – ground-thumping explosions, gunfire - could be heard sometimes, even through the glorious sound of the Gipsy Kings.

The militants went to war every day – they lived each day as their last. Aslan came to see me pretty often, making a short visit before he went to fight. I was begging him to bring me to the post office again and let me talk to my mom. Even if they took a pity on me and allow me to do so, it was not possible any more. After the storming of Grozny, the phone connection with Russia and the rest of the world was cut. The main post office building was bombed. Communications were down.

My presence there had come to a standstill – it seemed that I was being held in reserve. I still had value because they hoped to get the money after the war ended. But what if they lost their patience? What if the war never ended? I was afraid their plans could change at any moment. They would like me to forever disappear.

Real life was happening in the world outside – the thought of it constantly weighed on me. Here in the room, time had stopped. Life had stopped.

One day, the Gipsy Kings were forever silenced. The electricity was completely cut off. Loneliness, longing and emptiness filled my tiny world. I was alone, and all of the things that made up my past life were gone – now I had lost it all. My last link to it had been that cassette tape. I was untethered and alone.

I was sure that only one other person on Earth – my mom – shared the same feelings. There was no one to help me. I had to look inside myself for support, and for strength. I had to resist the forces around me and not let myself shatter like glass.

With the electricity gone, the nights were now black. The day would fade slowly into a darkness so deep, and so profound, that it made a mockery of my previous conceptions of what the word meant, or what the night was like. I was linked now to the pre-modern peoples, who huddled in fear of the darkness, and invented stories of monsters and demons who ruled the time between dusk and dawn.

At night, I peered into an existential nothingness. I felt like an insect, caught and placed in a dark box. These feelings of abandonment and the world's indifference to me were so strong that it seemed like I wasn't a person at all, but a phantom, and I simply did not exist.

I hated the gang and everyone in it.

Slowly, I came to understand that Aslan was the only one who might help me. His humanity towards me raised my hopes. There was a tiny invisible bond between us, and I was hoping that with time I could convince him to help me. I felt that he was enjoying our conversations, and he was interested in my personality. We had short meetings, just a few minutes a day, but I sensed that deep inside, he took pity on me. He was adamant about achieving their criminal purpose and getting the money, but he was also kind to me in his own way. After I fired the gun at the wall, the next day, he came into my room in a flurry. His eyes shone.

"I like your character, and you're beautiful. You're a warrior. True Vainakh"

He saw a fearless warrior in me, such as he was himself – someone for whom the war is an exciting game, tickling the nerves and chilling the spine. But he was wrong. I wasn't like that – I was trying to just survive. I did not want to play the fearless fighter. I wanted to go home.

He had been enthusiastically telling me stories about an elusive detachment of women snipers, the so-called "White Tights." They fought on the side of anti-Russian forces in war zones. In Chechnya, they were legends. No one knew who they were. Some people thought they were biathletes from the Baltic states - Lithuania, Latvia, and Estonia - three former Russian republics.

Female snipers, mercenaries – never seen, the sound of the kill shot the first hint of their presence - who had claimed the lives of many Russian troops. They were ruthless ghosts who never missed. They were hated, and they were feared. The only ones who ever saw their faces were the ones who killed them.

They refused to be caught alive. Faced with capture, they would shoot themselves in the head, believing that to die instantly was the greatest mercy. The White Tights left no clues behind them, no hint of who they really were. And nobody knew if they were reality or just a myth.

I could tell: Aslan wanted to believe they were real. And he wanted to believe that I was like them.

Once, they took me to shoot.

I was confused by such an attention, but endlessly happy to finally breathe the long-awaited fresh air. It was winter and a warm gray day – there was no sun at all. A large group came outside into the deserted and gloomy courtyard. There were eight men with me – all the familiar faces from inside the apartment. The winter chill went straight to my head like a drug, the oxygen saturating my pores. Despite the absence of sunlight, the gray and gloomy day brought me amazing pleasure – it made me want to run, far away from this terrible place, without looking back.

Everyone climbed into two cars parked at the entrance of the building. I watched in silence and listened to their conversations, trying to recognize familiar words in their bizarre language. We were in a suburb of Grozny with a few five story apartment buildings around. The trip was very short. Five minutes later, the car stopped, right at the side of the road. There was an uninhabited open landscape on both sides of the road, covered with dry and frozen ground, and the remnants of dry vegetation. On the horizon, I could see a forest belt consisting of gray leafless trees, naked for winter.

The militants unloaded the car, carrying weapons and boxes of targets out. They were cheerful. I watched this gang of heavily armed and laughing men under the low leaden sky and I could not understand how it happened that I was among them, helpless to change anything.

Suddenly there was deafening gunfire. One of the men tossed a glass bottle in the air, and several others volleyed at it with their machine guns. When the roar quieted down, the militant set a row of the green glass bottles on a small hill a few yards away. Aslan approached, with a pistol in his hand. He cocked the gun and gave it to me - it was large, black and heavy. I wished he had given me a machine gun. The weapon in my hand made me excited, the blood pumping in my veins.

My mom and dad were avid fishermen, mushroom pickers, and hunters. They both shared these hobbies with a passion. Each year, they would eagerly await the arrival of spring and summer to begin the season's outings into nature. Of course they took me with them. I didn't particularly enjoy these trips – the mushroom picking and fishing, and then spending the night in a tent – no thank you. I did not share their love of the "wild" weekends. I'm a city girl – I've always loved the comfort of the stone jungle.

The only part I enjoyed was the hunting. If my parents took me to hunt wild birds, I was endlessly happy. I have always loved to shoot. A weapon in my hand always evoked a sense of awe and euphoria in me.

Aslan indicated the glass bottles a few yards ahead of me.

"Can you shoot any of them?"

Holding the gun with both hands, I took aim and fired. The shots were loud and the gun had a strong recoil I didn't expect – I shuddered and cringed. My second shot obliterated one of the bottles, shrapnel spraying in all directions. In my excitement, I shot the rest of the bullets. Aslan reloaded the gun and gave it to me again. Calmer now, I took aim and fired more carefully.

BLAM! A bottle shattered.

BLAM! Another.

Within a few minutes, I had destroyed most of the bottles. I felt strong. I felt powerful.

When you hold a loaded gun in your hands, there is a special feeling. You know that the weapon is a powerful force, and its main purpose is to kill – an animal, another person, the gun doesn't care. And there is the concept of "self-defense," when you have the right to kill if your own life is in danger. I was in just such a situation, where I could have easily shot the men around me, and called it self-defense. How many of them would I be able to shoot before the survivors tore my body to pieces with machine gun fire? Maybe I could kill every one of them, turning eight people into a bloody mess, and then jump in the car, take a few pistols and rifles with me, and leave this terrible place forever. It would be carnage, like a scene from an action movie.

I glanced at the men around me. Real life doesn't work like a movie script. If this was my chance to escape, it wasn't a very convincing one.

It occurred to me that because of weakness or fear, I was not able to read the signs given to me from above. I did not use either chance sent to me so far. Were they really chances to escape, or were they tests?

* * *

Aslan reveled in the war.

The war was his passion – he was an implacable fighter who would never lay his arms down and would fight to the end. The death of his enemies had become the focus of his life. He told me horror stories of the war, the battles he had seen, and off hand cruelties and atrocities that were everyday events.

During the taking of the Dudayev Palace in Grozny, the Chechens had hung the crucified and decapitated corpses of Russian soldiers from the windows. According to Aslan, the Chechens beat their Russian prisoners, tortured them, executed them in public, cut their heads off, scalped them and skinned them alive – but these were reasonable responses to the excesses of Russian soldiers against the peaceful Chechen people and Chechen prisoners of war. From both sides there was fantastic brutality - I almost couldn't believe what I was hearing.

The war had attracted mercenaries from around the world, who were now flooding into the country. Some were Islamic mujahideen – the so-called holy warriors, who came to help the Muslim Chechens fight the godless Russians. For them, to die in battle was their highest wish – they would be with Allah in paradise before their corpses were even cold. Other fighters came for the excitement of war and to make money.

I panicked now whenever I heard someone entering from outside. The apartment would fill with male voices. I was gripped by despair. It seemed senseless to even remain alive. The new arrivals were not concerned if they lived or died – no, it was better for them to die surrounded by the corpses of their enemies. And I was their enemy. They cared nothing for this life. Their days were numbered anyway. Why wouldn't they use me as they wished, and then kill me?

"Don't knock on the door when the mujahideen are here," Aslan said, performing yet another kindness towards me, one that did not tally with the general concept of holding a hostage, or committing atrocities during a war. "They have their own rules about how to treat hostages."

So I would sit there, afraid to move, the mercenaries right outside my door. For my own safety, I would not make a single sound. Sometimes it seemed to me that Aslan would change his mind and let me go – maybe even help me escape the country. I did not understand his duplicity, and never stopped trying to persuade him to help me.

"Aslan, let me go. The war is going to last a long time. My mom doesn't have that kind of money. Your plan won't work. Just let me go."

He was silent. For a few seconds, he looked like he was about to agree, but the moment passed. Instead, he rubbed his beard and became the man with the sly fox face again. With a cruel smile, he said:

"You're going to be here as long as necessary."

I did not know how to convince him.

Yet friendship with Aslan brought me some advantages. I could wash my hair once a week and take a bottle-shower in the evenings, when he was one of the guards. The electricity and hot water were cut off, but there was still gas supplied to the apartment. Aslan would heat water on the stove for me, and I would mix it with cold water to wash my hair. I acquired a notebook and a pen from him – late at night, when I was unable to fall asleep, I drew by the light of a kerosene lamp.

One dark evening, Shorty opened the door and said with a sneer:

"Look who we have here!"

For a split second I assumed that *they* had finally come, and *they* were going to take me home. I nearly jumped when the next man appeared in the doorway. I was stunned. I was looking at the Italian.

"Do you remember your friend Italiano?"

He said the nickname with a disrespectful and mocking tone. I felt that Shorty was slightly humiliating him, and I was glad about that, even if it only seemed like it to me.

The return of the Italian called up unbearably painful emotions for me. The memories of that night surfaced in my mind as if they had happened the day before. It cut my heart open like a razor blade.

He was the only one of them I had known in my past life. In my happy life, when I was naïve and it seemed like the world was one big happy family, where we all loved each other and enjoyed each other. The past few months, I had tried to drive away the memories of my former life, so I would not go insane from anguish. I locked those memories deep inside me, and did not give myself permission to let them out. I couldn't handle it. And here was The Italian, the agent of my suffering - his presence made my heart shrink. I hated him.

I looked into his eyes in the dim light of the lamp.

"How much I hate you, Italian!"

He grinned. But it was not with the arrogance or confidence of previous days – he looked pathetic now. Now I was sure – the derogatory tone Shorty took with him was real, and there was some reason behind it.

The next day, when Aslan showed up, I tried to find out about the Italian. My feelings had not deceived me. The Italian was an absolute zero, a pawn in the game. During my kidnapping, his role was to follow me and find out the places I frequented.

No one respected him, and that made me glad in an evil and vindictive way. When the war started, he fled Chechnya and had been hiding somewhere outside the country. He was not considered Vainakh, and therefore everyone looked down on him. He had never even been to Europe – he simply created that illusion so people who didn't know him would think he was successful. I gloated and rejoiced that he was not recognized among his friends. Compared to mine, his suffering was miniscule, but it still made me happy.

January 1995
Astrakhan, Russia

"In connection with the start of military operations, all search activities in the territory of Chechnya have been postponed." – the words sounded like a verdict.

According to the federal officers, the war would end in a few weeks, and then the search would resume again.

The woman could not wait. The war was a bloodbath – that much was clear from the TV and the newspapers. They couldn't know when it was going to end, or how. There was no time to waste. Waiting for the war to end was waiting too long.

She wrote letters begging for help, to the Red Cross, the government and even the president. Endless days would pass while she waited for an answer – each time she opened the envelopes with trembling hands, her breath stuck in her throat, only to read, once again, the disappointing words: "The search will resume at the first opportunity."

The abductors no longer called.

Apprehension tortured her, causing the woman to assume the worst. Faith was the only thing left that helped her endure the long and painful days and nights.

She waited and prayed – sometimes, so long and so hard that she prayed herself into oblivion, until she lost consciousness. She disappeared from the real world, seeing apparitions, or maybe they were just dreams – she could not tell the difference. When she came back, she was amazed how clearly she remembered all the details of her strange travels. She entered into someone's unknown body and flew over the Earth. She watched the surroundings through someone else's eyes. She saw her daughter, and she knew that her daughter was alive. She felt it almost physically. The hallucinatory journeys were so confusing, but satisfying. They were feeding her.

She saw the Almighty, who appeared and spoke to her without words. He was fatherly - caring and incredibly calm, instilling a sense of hope in her and faith that her daughter was alive.

After these dreams and visions, she came back to the real world with an unwavering sense of confidence. What was happening on the other side fueled her. From that other world, she drew new strength to live on.

January 1995
Grozny, Chechnya

The nights became especially difficult – the impenetrable darkness lit only by a kerosene burner, that made everything seemed even more eerie. As each endless night came in, I turned into a cave dweller. The room became my tomb. January came to an end – If I had a calendar, I could cross the fourth month of my captivity out of my life.

It was wasting away – minute by minute, I was losing it pointlessly. My situation had been bad enough, but the war made it so much worse. A gang of thugs had kidnapped me in the hope of a quick and easy score, but they had miscalculated badly. My mother didn't have the money they wanted, and they didn't foresee the arrival of a protracted and brutal war. Although, it was possible that they were well informed about it, long before its arrival.

The Chechen army consisted of many different units and groups, large and small. Each was supposed to report to an assigned field commander, but some groups didn't obey anyone. They committed acts of sabotage, or pursued their own criminal ends – the sale of weapons, drugs, and slaves, as well as trafficking people in and out of the country. The war gave them cover and a pretext for their actions.

I guessed they didn't know what to do with me now. To make public phone calls to Russia from the ruined city, under the constant threat of falling mortar shells – that wasn't an option. The main post office building was bombed and destroyed long ago. Russian troops were moving deeper into the country and occupying cities and towns. The losses on both sides were enormous.

I was lucky. My captors were religious fanatics. They didn't smoke or drink alcohol – I never heard a drunken brawl or a feast. How much more horrible it would have been with heavily-armed drunk men in the apartment, angry and holding a hostage in the next room. I would not have survived a week.

In moments of despair, I dreamed that a bomb would fall right onto this apartment, and smash the whole thing to hell, with me in it. My perpetual fear of the unknown was leading to a desire for someone to end this miserable existence. I drove away my own thoughts of suicide – in my heart I still hoped to leave here one day – but what a relief it would be for all this to just suddenly… stop. Every time I thought out all kinds of options for salvation and convinced myself that it would happen soon. But I also did not know how much longer I could stand this existence.

I comforted myself with the thought that I would sooner or later be swapped in a prisoner of war exchange. Or the Russians would eventually capture the whole of Chechnya, so it would be easier for me to find the way out. Or there would be someone – some compassionate local – who would report the location of the captive to the Russian authorities. I was not even close to my goals. My dreams of escape were just that – daydreams.

Left alone in the room, I was able to live in a fantasy, waiting for rescue or some elaborate escape. During the past few months, I had been able to somehow adapt to the conditions imposed on me. It was a temporary arrangement, designed to help me survive this time, and not go insane or kill myself.

The small gang of ten people, who I had come to know by face, was growing and changing. A few had died, and others had been wounded and could no longer fight. I became accustomed to seeing the same people again and again, especially Aslan, who seemed more or less good-natured. I had learned the demeanor of each of them. I could distinguish their voices and footsteps through the door.

But then the new faces appeared. The new people brought new fears. My heart would stop at the sight of the bearded and unkempt mujahideen. There were only a few of them – there was no mercy in them at all, and perhaps no humanity. Their eyes were blank and hard – they had come here to kill and to die, if that was Allah's will. They spoke yet another indecipherable language. I could not understand a word they said, but I could feel the cruelty emanating from them.

Sometimes one of them would open the door to my room, stand at the threshold, and stare at me. I would pretend to be asleep, my body motionless on the bed, my face to the wall. I couldn't move. Inside I would shake in terror – I hoped that he could not see me trembling. I just prayed that soon the door would close, and I would be left alone. The fear settled inside me, and I could not overcome it. It was rapidly destroying me.

***

Outside, the night came, and impenetrable darkness enveloped my already hopelessly gloomy room. Behind the door there were voices and laughter. In the pitch black I lay on the bed, my head covered with a pillow, trying to fall asleep, just so I wouldn't have to hear the ominous sounds behind the wall. More than anything, I was irritated by their cheerful mood.

My brain refused to relax, and my racing heartbeat would not let me sleep. My ear was trained by now – even muted by the pillow, I could recognize all of the sounds in the apartment. Suddenly I heard a painfully familiar rustle. Someone cranked the key in the lock. I held my breath.

A man entered the room and closed the door behind him. Footsteps quietly approached. I no longer pressed the pillow over my ears. Now I listened – I listened with my entire body, my whole being. I could hear the distinct sound of a kerosene lamp placed on the floor.

I sat up, pushing the pillow aside. A circle of eerie yellow light came from the lantern, pushing the darkness to the corners. In its sinister glow, *he* came straight toward me. He was rank with the smell of unwashed flesh. His eyes seemed to glare red with hellfire, his face framed by a jungle of overgrown black hair.

I could not distinguish the features of his face – he was huge black mass, coming right at me, unbuttoning his pants on the way. He didn't say a word.

I was engulfed by a fire from inside my body – it was fight or flight, but there was nowhere to run. Adrenaline surged through my system. Terror kicked into gear something I never expected – aggression. I didn't even wait for him to reach me. I attacked.

I jumped out of the bed and into the corner of the room. I picked up the tape recorder – my salvation for so long but useless now that the electricity was cut – and threw it at him. As if that could even slow him down. He was a monster – the recorder bounced off his chest and fell to the floor.

He kept coming, his face blank, eyes like the living dead. I kicked him and punched at him. I couldn't see anything in front of me, just my arms, my knees and feet, flying forward, churning, striking at this huge mass of flesh. I attacked him with everything I had – all of the helplessness of my existence mobilized and directed at this one target.

The two of us were like one big tangle – a twisted mass of anger and venom, cruelty and hate. No cry for help escaped from me – I silently fought with all my being, and I did not care if I lived through it. A sudden sharp slap across my face burned my skin like hellfire, and threw me backwards. I hit the wall and fell onto the floor.

I seemed to lose consciousness and become immersed in a black empty abyss, just for a split second. An instant later I woke up, rushing again into the unequal battle. But I was no longer able to do it. I was on the floor, my hands restrained over my head, my body crushed under the weight of this disgusting brute. I could not move, could not breathe, and was just trying to dodge my face from the foul rank breath of the mujahid. I sobbed silently, the salty tears flowing into my mouth.

The huge body moved on top of me, trying to satisfy its pleasure, violently tearing my flesh from the inside. I felt no pain – I just wanted it to end. Finally, the man's body trembled. His animal desire satiated, he weakened. A moment later, he got up, and I started breathing again.

Without a word, he left the room, leaving me alone, humiliated and disgraced, torn to pieces. My lips were bleeding, left wrist was covered in blood, but I still did not feel any physical pain. A strong sense of aversion filled me.

I pulled the pillowcase off the pillow and began to carefully wipe away the traces of his alien and stinking residue from between my legs. I jumped up and down, trying to drive the last remnants of him from my body.

I was crushed, flat and dead, as if someone had ripped my soul out and there was nothing left inside but emptiness. And yet, even in the immediate aftermath, even while in shock, my desire to escape remained powerful. It was still there – I could feel it.

I wouldn't let this destroy me. Despite everything, I would not allow myself to lose my mind.

* * *

In my world, I had no friends.

I was one person, alone among my enemies. But there are moments in life that a person cannot survive by herself. I had reached my limit. I could not handle anything more. I wanted to believe that Aslan was brought into my life for a reason. Without his help, I wasn't going to make it. Whatever feelings Aslan had for me, I needed him to act on them now – he was the most compassionate and kind among them all.

All this time, I had suffered and cried alone. But now my faith in my own strength was shaken. I could not withstand the next onslaught – and I was on the verge of insanity.

The next night Aslan came to my room. I was waiting for him and I could not resist. For the first time, I cried in front of him, desperately cried for his help. I broke down. I begged and I threatened him. I sobbed like a child and I yelled in despair.

"I'm going to kill myself!"

I did not know what effect it had on him. He was impossible to read. Maybe it was a coincidence, and he had been making efforts on my behalf all along. Or maybe he finally took pity on my plight right then.

He smoothed his beard staring through me with his foxy grin.

"You will be moved tomorrow, to another place," he said. "You're leaving in the morning. There, you will be safe."

For a moment, I was positive that a guardian angel was watching over me. Aslan couldn't let me go or help me escape, but at least I would be far from this place.

Somehow I had penetrated into the heart of this man. I felt sure that sooner or later he would help me get home.

I could not sleep, thinking about where I would be the next day. I didn't care – I just wanted to leave this gloomy apartment. There was no way to escape from it. I tried to drive away the thoughts of hopelessness, in order to keep my sanity. I had to have faith. I listened to the sounds behind the wall, lying in the dark on the bed waiting and ready to leave at any moment. Dawn had not yet come when I heard a furtive movement outside my room.

Aslan came in without making a sound, lighting his way with a burning candle. He always moved quickly and silently. As if he was on the prowl. He not only looked like a fox, he had the same habits as one. I was ready. Aslan sat on the edge of the bed, and even the old bed didn't creak under him. He stroked his beard as always and his eyes gleamed in the dim light. In the air, I felt a weight – this moment was important. I froze in frustration:

"Something has changed? I'm staying here?"

He shook his head. "No. Just calm down. I made a promise to you, and I will fulfill it. But I want to warn you. As a friend."

He looked like a cold-blooded killer once again. Mercy was replaced by the cruelty in his eyes.

"This is for your own good. During the trip, if we run into a Russian checkpoint, you'd better sit quietly, or better, pretend to be asleep. If you cry or ask for help… it will be bad. They will start a shootout and you'll be the first one to die. Your mother will also die. I can't do more for you than tell you this."

For the first time in the many days and nights of my captivity, I felt somewhat happy, if only for a short while. It was a relief to be taken away from that terrible place, which will forever leave an ugly scar in my soul. I was as grateful for Aslan's care as the abused and hungry dog is grateful when he is thrown a piece of bread. It was my small victory. My soul was tormented, but I continued to live, no matter what.

I did not need much time to get ready – all of my meager possessions would fit in two hands. Except for the pink robe, which was bulky and heavy, but I did not want to part with it. It was warm and cozy. Although now I only wore the long blue dress, sometimes I used the warm robe – when it was cold. I packed it in the plastic bag together with the black square of my old, folded mini-dress, which I had kept under the pillow until now. It took me about a minute to get my other belongings together – a few hygiene items, which had been a real treasure for me.

I had been ready to leave the night before, and now was looking forward to this exciting moment. I could not see myself in the mirror, but I could easily imagine my strange appearance. If not paying attention to my light green eyes, I could easily pass for a local woman. The long blue dress covered my body, and my blond hair was hidden under a headscarf. At the moment I did not care much about my looks – I could not wait to leave this godforsaken unfortunate place from which there was nowhere to go except the cemetery. I hoped that new place might bring me a chance to escape. I wanted to believe.

Aslan led me out of the dark apartment, through the even darker hallway, and outside to the green military SUV that was parked, already started up, in front of the building. There were men inside the vehicle – a driver and Shorty. The rear seat was taken by me and Aslan.

Once again, I was driven in a car into the unknown. I sat by the window, leaning my forehead against the cool glass. Outside, it was very dark, but I felt the approach of dawn. I watched as we left the suburbs, leaving behind a few of Khruschev's five-story apartment buildings, the old hulks flowing backwards and disappearing into the darkness. The car bounced up and down on the pot-holed road, not giving me a second to relax and soak up the serene beauty of the pre-dawn. I missed the world terribly, and I looked with pleasure out the window, trying to catch a glimpse of open nature. I didn't know when, or if, I would ever see it again.

Spring was approaching. Outside the window there was a glimmer of dawn. Life went on, and what happened was not up to me. The great Chechen land was pockmarked, burned, and ripped by bomb explosions and massive gunfire.

In the midst of so much destruction, who would care about a single, lost, tortured soul?

I was torn by two opposites. On the one hand, if I tried to shout for help at the military checkpoint, I might be saved. On the other hand, if I did that, I might cause a gunfight and then I would just be killed. The militants were moving from one place to another under the guise of innocent civilians. I could tell by the way they looked. None of them carried an exposed weapon. I guessed that I was with them in the car playing the role of someone's wife or sister.

The excitement overwhelmed me. What should I do? What if this was a chance? What if it was my *last* chance?

The trip was very long – about an hour or more. At dawn, the blurred landscapes outside the window began to turn into three-dimensional objects. On both sides of the road there were sparsely growing trees, with foggy mountains on the horizon. The wild country around us was dark gray – the trees had not blossomed yet. We passed a lone house from time to time – they all seemed empty and abandoned. The people had fled deeper into the countryside to escape the war.

I was tense now. The car rolled quickly on the bumpy side roads in the gloomy dawn, as I prayed to be stopped by a military patrol. My heart beat crazily. I was ready to explode and didn't even consider pretending to be asleep. On the contrary, my eyes were wide open, scanning for movement, for soldiers, for anything. I had decided, for myself, for everyone – I would scream for help at the first Russian army checkpoint. For once, my actions would seal all of our fates.

Time passed, and nothing was happening. The militants kept quiet, not speaking a word. The gray morning did not get any lighter. Everything was shrouded in a thick, ominous fog. The spirit of war was in the air and made it heavy. Would I manage to survive this nightmare? When would it be over? And how would it end?

CHAPTER SIX

March 1995
Gurchuloy, Chechnya

Soon, the car entered a village. The vehicle moved slowly along the muddy narrow road between rows of tightly packed houses. I was struck by the high green iron fences. The homes stood close to each other and each house was protected by one of these iron barriers. Each of the fences was connected to the next, almost all of them painted green, and this made it seem like we were driving past one long wall of solid iron. Behind them, I could just see the roofs of the houses, covered with slate. From the ground to three feet up, everything was caked in dark gray dirt. I could only guess what was going on behind the high iron railings.

The car stopped in front of one of the houses. Shorty jumped out of the car and quickly ran to the entrance. After a moment, the huge gates creaked open. The sound was loud, a shrieking of metal scraping the ground. Shorty pushed each one aside and let the car in. Once the car was inside the yard, he slammed them shut again. They were tall – much taller than he was. Once again, I was separated from the rest of the world, swallowed this time by a green iron monster.

Hidden behind the massive fence, there was a nice red brick house, surrounded by a large yard. A woman appeared at the threshold of the house, in a long dress with her hair covered. She looked imperious, like she was the ruler of this place. Our eyes met through the window glass and I saw no kindness in them. Aslan's behavior and attitude towards me always changed, depending on who else was around. He was kind and compassionate when we were alone – I had been able to discover his hidden humanity during the past few weeks. But he was absolutely ruthless among other people. He turned to me and snapped:

"Get out of the car!"

The yard was full of people. The woman, Aslan and Mirza led me inside the house. They talked among themselves in their own language while I stood waiting. I looked around the yard – if only I could convince Aslan to help me to escape. This town did not seem that wild, or isolated – I might be able to find my way from here. This move could be a good sign.

The house had no electricity. Like a huge octopus, the war had spread its tentacles everywhere. I followed the other three up the steps, down a dark corridor, into a kitchen dominated by a large wooden table. We passed through the kitchen into a room with sofas covered by colorful coverlets. The walls were decorated with woven Turkish rugs. The windows were covered with two layers of heavy drapes pushed to the sides. Underfoot I felt a soft pile wool carpet. It felt like home here – someone else's. It was going to be my prison.

The next room seemed like someone's bedroom. The windows were flanked by delicate white curtains of sheer lace, the bed covered by a quilted bedspread, and there were colorful carpets on the walls and on the floor. After months of observing the ugly premises of the previous place, this home seemed loved and taken care of. The owners of the house were most likely a wealthy family.

The door from this bedroom led to the back of the house. A small dark corridor led me to the most distant part of the house, where there was a tiny room, something like an oversized storage. It would be very dark in there, if not for a narrow window which let the morning light in. I realized immediately that this room was the end point – the place where I would stay.

After a moment, I was left there alone.

The window was very narrow, as if it specially made to prevent the escape of a prisoner. However, I could look through it at a section of the yard. After the monotony of the apartment in Grozny, where I couldn't see anything through the black paint on the windows, looking through this window was like watching an anthill. From where I stood, I could see the yard, with the summer kitchen enclosed by netting. Several fighters were sitting on the ground, resting. One woman was busy at the stove and setting the table. On the right, in the distance I could see the wattle and daub of the bathroom. I could see what I guessed was the well, and behind it a pile of firewood stacked near the fence. The yard was big, and continued even further – out of my sight.

Fortunately, even the narrow slit window let in quite a bit of light. It was nice to see natural daylight and watch how the morning came in.

Along the opposite wall from the window, there was a single bed. It seemed very old, with twisted iron bars at the head and at the foot. Exactly the same bed was once in my grandmother's house. The bed was in my bedroom when I was 4 or 5 years old. At that time, the mattress was on a large iron grid that always creaked.

I did not like to sleep alone. Grandma came into my room every night when I stayed at her house, and lay down close to me on the narrow bed. She told me fairytales and stories that she composed herself. She spoke in a low and soothing voice and waited for me to fall asleep. Then she probably went to her own bedroom, but I had no idea about this, because in the morning she came back and woke me up. My grandma's house was warm and always smelled delicious. In my grandmother's house there were a few large, covered fireplaces that were used to warm the place. They were made of stones, and went all the way to the ceiling, with tiny doors at the floor level where you could insert firewood. My grandfather was a fireplace builder by profession. In the winter, coming into the house from outside, it was so nice to lean against the warm fireplace and cuddle up in blankets, listening to the crackle of the burning firewood.

Now, this bed reminded me of those distant times when I felt loved and protected. It was covered with a red satin coverlet.

A small bedside table between the wall and the bed, and a kerosene lamp on the table completed the set up. Two red pieces of carpet covered the floor. A patterned carpet hung over the bed. If it wasn't a prison cell, it would be quite a comfortable room. The only things missing were a tape recorder and a Gipsy Kings cassette.

I sat on the bed, looking around. My body was still sore and aching after the fight with the Mujahideen. But I was very happy that I had left that sinister tomb. Even the pain seemed to me quite tolerable. After months in a dark and gloomy prison, this place was bright and somehow cozy. The carpets on the walls and on the floor created a sense of home. It wasn't even a full room – only half of it, with a leftover window. Some time ago this place had been separated by that wall, installed in the middle of what had once been a larger room. I couldn't think of another explanation for the odd shape and window placement.

I tried to convince myself that I could escape from here – it would probably be easier than from the last place.

Aslan came and left a large piece of pita bread and a three-liter jar of canned fruit. It seemed like he knew the house well, so I showered him with questions about it.

It turned out that the house belonged to the family of Mirza. Shorty himself, his mother, father, and younger sister lived there. His older brother, who had recently died in the war, had lived there too. Shorty's family provided the summer house, in the yard, for the use of militants and mercenaries.

I was shocked by the idea that I was a prisoner in someone's home, with the cooperation of someone's family. How strong the hatred for Russians must be if the mother and father have allowed a hostage held in their own home.

I was encouraged when Aslan told me that no one would touch me while I was here. Of course I doubted that Shorty would agree with this opinion, being the owner of the house.

I would have to adapt to new conditions. The most difficult part seemed to be establishing my own semblance of a life and a schedule. I would need to find access to a toilet, and the wash basin.

My thoughts were interrupted by sounds coming from outside. A voice called, cutting through the silence, almost singing. There was something beautiful about it, and I sat listening, fascinated. It was the first time I heard the Muslim call to prayer – the muezzin cried from minaret.

Cautiously, I looked out the little window. The militants began to prepare. There were a few of them, and I studied them through the narrow glass as they stopped whatever they were doing and readied themselves to give glory to their God. They all stood in the same direction and started to pray, oblivious to everything else. There was beauty and a strange attraction in that humble service.

What did they ask of Allah? Did they pray for forgiveness? Was their guilty conscience tormented because they had warped someone's innocent life?

Living behind a locked door, side by side with the militants for months, I never had a chance to encounter their traditions. No wonder – I wasn't staying with them as a student traveler to learn their way of life. I was their prisoner. The only feature of their lives I became familiar with, which I had to face and accept, was to use a pitcher to clean myself when I went to the bathroom.

Now I could watch them closely, and witness all that they did.

They were ardent followers of their religion and patriots of their country. During the Second World War, the Russian people had defended their country against the attacks of fascism. It hadn't occurred to anyone to condemn them for it. Why had the Russian government decided that such a freedom-loving people as the Chechens would surrender without a fight, and would welcome an invasion from the outside?

They would fight while they were still alive. Or until the ones for whom the war was profitable ceased receiving dividends from all the blood.

Suddenly the door opened and there was Mirza. He was unarmed. I backed away from the window, and prepared to take his taunts. He leaned on the stately iron headboard.

"Listen carefully," he said. "There are new rules. You will be able to go out of this room three times a day – in the morning, at midday and in the evening. You'll be called when it's time, so stick to the schedule. You won't be here for long. Behave calmly and politely."

He enjoyed his newfound importance. I thought back to how he had tortured me with his words, and to my humiliation at being struck by him.

"I would like to go out now. Can I?"

He shook his head. "It's not time yet. Later."

Why did I even think about asking him this question! If he wasn't able to threaten me with a gun in my face in this house, then he would certainly choose another convenient way to humiliate me. Once again, he hurt my feelings, and he did it masterfully.

Outside the window the morning came – bright and sunny – one of those that's supposed to fill you with joy and happiness. Sun broke over the horizon and lit up the whole Earth with the power and energy of the new day. The warm rays of light penetrated through the small window and forced my eyes to squint. How I would love to go right now, into the new day with an open heart and dive into the freshness of the morning, to wash my face with cool dew and wake up from my long nightmare. But my relationship with the world had been violated and knocked askew – a new sunny day no longer overwhelmed me with creative energy, but instead made me suffer from poisonous helplessness and bitterness.

I looked out the window. I watched the life and concerns of other people through the glass – like I was living their lives instead of my own. In my previous place of confinement, in the isolation of the black room, I could keep aloof and live in my own thoughts, dreams and memories. This place was turning out to be more brutal – it was unbearable to see that the world had not collapsed, but continued on with me simply deleted from it.

I wanted my own life back. I wanted freedom.

Here, there were no war sounds – it was if there was not a war at all. Only the group of bearded Mujahideen outside in the yard reminded me that somewhere very near, the bloodshed continued.

I still had enough luck to get out into the fresh again – very briefly.

The key in the lock turned and Shorty opened the door. He was back. I had not heard his footsteps – the carpets on the floor hid the noise from me.

"Let's go now," he said.

He ordered me, rather than told me. Any action was better than sitting and grieving over my unhappy fate, and I had to explore my new routine and the way to the toilet.

I followed Shorty back through the tiny dark hallway, through the small cozy bedroom, and the large room with sofas and carpets. All the rooms were drowned in the sunlight pouring through the large windows. I wondered if there were iron grills on windows. From the hall he led the way into the kitchen. This time, I noticed a few rooms located to the left of the kitchen. One of them looked like a dining room. Shorty took me out the same way that we came in during the early morning – to the right, through a dark corridor and outside onto the porch.

A fresh and warm breeze blew in my face, enveloped me, and carried me away for a moment into distant memories. There, when we traveled as a family on a snow white ship, down the river during one of our summer vacations. There, when we were standing on the deck and a warm wind blew over our faces with pleasant river air as we sailed past breathtaking landscapes. Back then the happiness had no limits.

The yard was crowded. The tall green iron fence securely hid what was happening. Next to the gate there was a car – a military jeep, the one I was brought in. The summer house was full of militants.

I already knew where the toilet was - from my little window I could see the gray structure of the latrine. I tried not to look at the people - I didn't want to attract even the slightest attention. I walked without making a single sound. I glanced around rapidly, keeping my head down as I moved toward the toilet. Shorty went ahead, leading the way, and turned around the corner of the house.

"Here is the wash basin."

The wash basin was attached to the wall, and next to it, there was a huge barrel, filled to the brim with water. Its top was open and a pipe extended down to it, collecting rainwater from the roof.

The women were washing clothes in a large basin. This was the back of the house, which was completely hidden and not visible from my tiny window.

On the ground there was a row of vessels. I picked up one – I already knew the routine. Now I had learned the path that I would walk three times a day, if I was lucky.

After a while, Shorty took me back through the house to my room and turned the key in the lock.

Long hours in anguish and loneliness dragged by.

During the past six months I had been sick from memories of the past. I lay still, in the grips of an acute homesickness. I was overcome by malaise, a way I had never been in my life. So vivacious, so carefree, so young so in love with life – that was the Lena I knew. But now the present was lost to me – I could barely move, I could barely carry out the simplest act. I only survived by dreaming of the future.

To my credit, I didn't let feelings of hopelessness destroy me. I pressed on, I persisted. I constantly thought about my mom – of how much I loved her, of so many good times we'd had in the past, of our reunion and the good times we would have in the future. We would remain side by side, inseparable, until the end of our days.

But each time I thought of her, it felt like a little bit more of my soul bled from my body. I would turn white from all the bleeding. She did not know if I was alive, and she was going through these months as alone as I was. I knew her character – she would not find solace in human pity, so she would suffer in solitude. These thoughts hurt me, and my emotional torture was such that it turned into physical pain. I felt a sharp ache in my chest, like a butcher's knife had penetrated my sternum and cut out not just my heart, but also my lungs. It seemed that I could no longer breathe.

Sometimes I really did feel that I was dying. I would lie in bed for hours and think it: "I'm dying."

It didn't make sense. Dying of what? Of cancer? Of heart disease?

No, not heart disease, but heartbreak. In those moments, I would be happy to die. To simply wither away, diminish, fall asleep and never wake up – it seemed like the best thing that could happen. But then the feeling would fade – it might take hours or days – and I would begin to return to something I could recognize as myself.

I was still here, still alive, and that meant I must press on, find a way to adapt, to survive, and maybe one day, escape into sunlight and safety and freedom.

* * *

The days looked exactly the same, and replaced each other one by one. Even after the long months in prison, I couldn't stop thinking about salvation – whether it came as an escape, or rescue from the outside. I believed that the day would come.

I needed a plan and an accomplice. I needed Aslan.

I couldn't do it without him. Hoping for the police to arrive was a dead end. They never turn up in the midst of an apocalypse to save one person – they would wait for the end of the war. I couldn't wait – I had to leave.

At dawn, the guttural voice of the muezzin echoed over the surrounding area from the tower of the minaret – the early morning call to prayer. The militants stopped what they were doing, and began to perform ritual ablutions – they washed their faces, hands and feet, and rolled up their trouser legs to mid-calf.

They prayed for the salvation of their souls several times a day. If I saw them praying in the courtyard through my window, I always watched the process carefully – the militants lined up neatly in a row, kneeling, prostrating, standing, moving in unison, an amazing display of the togetherness and intimacy and brotherhood of the Muslim people.

Aslan came to see me almost every evening.

Mostly, he stayed for just a few minutes. Sometimes he was able to stay longer and, increasingly, he was willing to answer my questions. It seemed to me he enjoyed my company. I found out that he lived in the same village, and was friends with Shorty since their childhoods. They were both 25.

Through Aslan, I got hold of a book, which made me unspeakably happy – now I could kill time. I asked him to bring me any book, the thickest he could find. He brought me "Crime and Punishment," by Dostoevsky, which he chose from the modest library of Mirza's family.

When I was in school, we tried in vain to understand the meaning of this difficult psychological novel. I didn't finish reading it then – it was too weird and tedious for my taste. But I did not mind trying my luck again.

Aslan would quietly creep to my room, scratching at the door, coming in with a smirk on his face, into the dark room, lit dimly by the kerosene lamp. He sat down carefully, one leg tucked underneath, leaning against the open metal headboard, as he told me stories about the war.

He also asked me about my life, and my childhood. I saw he was enjoying his time with me – more so with each passing day. If not for the fact that he was one of the terrorists, I could have considered him my spiritual friend.

Anytime I told him about my life before captivity, it made my imprisonment feel all the more acute by bringing back my sweet and dear memories of the past. I could not hold back and wept in front of him.

"Let me go, Aslan. Our family does not have the money. You will never get the ransom. It makes no sense to keep me here. Please, let me go."

He comforted me as a big brother or a friend, but he was adamant. I begged him to help me to escape, but he always answered the same:

"You're not *my* prisoner. I don't have the power to decide."

I was not the only one kidnapped and held in Chechnya. Aslan told me heart-rending stories about the other hostages. Brutal stories about how the Chechen militants cut off the heads of the hostages, skewered them on stakes and put them on public display to intimidate the others.

He told me about a concentration camp that was operating in one of the villages, a story which brought me to tears. Prisoners who no one gave a ransom for were forced to build roads. Many of them were tortured in front of the others to create a climate of fear. Some of the "unwanted" were simply shot.

Aslan told stories of the horrors of the war, and the fate of the prisoners of war and hostages – it plunged me into shock – I could expect the same fate for myself.

But according to him, the most inhuman and bloodthirsty villains of his stories were, of course, the Russian troops. He talked about the torture and mass killings of innocent Chechen civilians, abuse of detainees, and the burning of houses – all done by Russians. The outrages would begin immediately after they took a village. The murder of innocent people was swift and terrible – punishment for the continued resistance of the Chechen fighters.

A war – it was the cruelest thing in the world.

Their war was large-scaled, violent, and bloody, coupled with pain, misfortune and loneliness. They were fighting for freedom and ideology.

My war was the struggle of one soldier, and also coupled with pain, misfortune and loneliness. And I was fighting for freedom and survival.

I was no longer afraid of Aslan. The more I saw him, the more I brought up the topic of my escape. I jokingly tried to discuss a plan that I could carry out with his help, gently probing the soil.

"What if you left the gate unlocked? Do you think that would work? I could try to silently go out the gate unnoticed in the dark on the way back from the bathroom."

I offered him humorous escape options, trying to catch his mood about it.

He brushed aside each of the options I offered him, but he didn't reject the overall idea of an escape. He played along with me, and for each idea I gave him, he gave me a good reason why it would never work. Our game amused him.

"You wouldn't get too far. Outside of these gates, there are a hundred more houses just like this one. You will be noticed immediately and caught. You will be sold to Wahhabis as a slave, or beheaded in the public square. There are a lot of people around here who would love to avenge their lost loved ones."

I wanted to believe that Aslan wasn't just trying to scare me, but was also trying to find the right way out. He wanted to help me, only he couldn't admit it right now.

I didn't know the location of the house, but I couldn't hear the sound of the war. The front had not yet reached this village. The militants would leave the premises in small groups of three or four people, and then would come back. The gates opened manually – the sound was unpleasant and lingered in the air afterward. Aslan went to fight mostly in the daytime. I never knew if he would come back in the evening.

He always came back.

I finished reading the Dostoevsky. The book was a dark philosophical argument about the conscience, sin and redemption. The main point was that, for whatever reason, the offender has committed a crime (especially murder), and must be punished, serving life in prison to suffer and repent of their deeds.

* * *

The women of the house were everywhere and nowhere at the same time. They appeared suddenly and silently, like ghosts, and disappeared just as quietly. I felt their presence in everything, but I rarely saw their faces. I often saw them from the back, quickly scurrying around the yard – they were busy preparing food, doing household chores, and cleaning. They never sat at the dining table under the tent with the men.

Shorty's mother was a little woman – nimble and plump. His sister was a thinner version of her mother – the way she walked and moved was the same, and her physique was the same, but she was more petite. Both wore long dresses and handkerchiefs tied around their heads, with their hair tucked underneath. I fleetingly encountered the mother in the kitchen a few times. I wanted to talk with one of the women and maybe ask for help, but I could not find an opportunity.

Since they were female, I thought I could find a way to appeal to reason. But they didn't pay any attention to me – I was totally ignored. They showed neither pity nor interest. I could even understand it a bit – they had the fresh wound of losing a son and a brother at the hands of the Russian army.

Still, Shorty's mother was an almost imperceptible, but undeniable, part of my life. Every day, she woke at dawn and immediately set to work. Through Aslan, I asked permission from her, as the mistress of the house, to have a chance to wash my hair and take a shower. My request was accepted. On the appointed evening, Shorty took me into the place - a small extension at the back of the house. Someone warmed the water for me and carefully brought it into the shower in a bucket. I filled another bucket with cold water from a huge rainwater barrel near the shower cabin, by myself.

I poured the warm and pleasant water from the bucket on my body, using a small can – very carefully and neatly, trying to enjoy the limited water a small amount at a time.

At such moments of simple human happiness, even if it's fleeting, everything that was outside the thin shower walls ceased to exist. The lukewarm water flowed from the top of my head right through the goose bumps all over my body, down to my feet. The whole process was uncomfortable, but at the same time, it was beautiful. I exposed my body and I bared my soul, greedily gasping for water.

The water had the magical ability to wash the mental stress away, if only for a few moments.

Now I felt like I was able to breathe again, and go on living.

I was grateful for the opportunity to take a shower and also, a scarf that Shorty's mother passed to me through Shorty. I did not know this woman, but I wanted to believe that she was sorry for me in her heart. I was trying to convince myself there are no people without compassion.

* * *

Outside my window, it rained for a few days in a row. The gray dust of the yard turned into brown mud.

Early morning, Mirza brought me back into the house after my usual trip the bathroom. I was in my dress, soaked by the torrential downpour outside. His mother was in the kitchen, preparing food. She said a couple of words to Shorty in Chechen, and he said something to her in response.

She glanced at me. For the second time I met her eyes – the first time was when I thought her evil eyes burned me through the glass of the car window, on the day when they brought me here.

"You can sit here," she said.

She spoke Russian. I was surprised by the timbre of her voice – it was low, masculine, and with a thick accent. She spoke quietly and pointed to a stool in the corner. Shorty went out into the corridor, leaving wet footprints from his boots on the wooden kitchen floor.

I took her words as an invitation to stay in the kitchen with her, in the place that was her kingdom. I sat down very gingerly on the stool, and stared at her in the gray light coming from the window on this wet and nasty morning.

Her tired and weathered face was lined with deep wrinkles. A bright kerchief was tied around her head very low, almost covering her dark and bushy eyebrows. She quickly sifted flour through a sieve. She did everything so fast that it seemed she was born with these skills or had done it all a million times. Her strong, work-worn hands quickly kneaded the dough with habitual gestures.

She covered the entire table with white flour, and her face a mask of concentration, started to roll out thin layers of dough. She placed them on each other, smudging butter between each layer. As if by magic, before my eyes she turned the dough into a big round layered pita, ready to bake. It was not simple cooking. What I observed was an art at which she was a master.

Shorty came back for me and took me out of the kitchen.

* * *

The kerosene lamp slowly smoked the room, illuminating a space around itself in yellow and warm light. At nightfall, all human feelings are more intense. The world outside the window became silent and lived its mysterious life.

I looked at the man sitting in front of me. With time, during our brief meetings, I began to understand Aslan – he was cruel, uncompromising, and strong. He was wild, with medieval manners. But he was also somehow merciful. His language was economical. Even while telling a story, he used few words. He spoke in the simplest possible language, without flourishes of any kind. Was it because he didn't have enough of the Russian language, or because of the peculiarities of the Chechen character?

It was time for the night prayer. Aslan left the room and returned in a few minutes later, his trouser legs rolled up to his mid-calves, barefoot, with the prayer rug under his arm. He did not say a word to me, but I knew what he was going to do.

He spread the mat on the floor, then directed his attention toward Mecca, in adoration of Allah, and began to pray in front of me. In the twilight of the kerosene lamp, his movements fascinated me. He began standing, then bowed, straightened up again, and then fell to his knees in prostration, with his forehead touching the ground. He produced mysterious hands movements, and then touched his face.

He whispered delightfully in prayer, and it seemed that this was the highest level of
intimacy – he was revealing himself to me. Either he thought I was a close friend, or he wanted me to become one. I did not share his faith in this being Allah – I no longer knew what I believed in. But I could see

the profound splendor in his relationship with this god, or demon, or figment of his own imagination – it ennobled him, and perhaps was the source of his undeniable courage. I watched him in awe, silently sitting on the bed, soaking in his peace and enjoying the simple grace of his movements and the beauty of what was happening.

What are you showing me, Aslan? Why are you inviting me to witness this?

* * *

It had been more than six months since I was last home. Six long months.

I was cut off from the familiar world so long ago that I had begun to get used to the local way of life. The existence of a captive gradually dominated my consciousness – my life was determined by my environment. I had to somehow organize my life, even being in the prison. A person is able to endure all that she faces except death. My consciousness built a barricade around itself and no longer let fear or any emotion get through it. The will to live, the strongest human instinct, adapted to any conditions. The constant feeling of despair eventually dulled and blocked the stress and forced me to live in spite of everything. I was carried on the waves of my worthless life like a ship without sails, driven by the wind, with no resistance. Day after day and month after month – so passed my life – in chains and shackles.

Aslan told me a little about the war. Both sides were suffering heavy casualties. Russian forces were seizing the large settlements – town by town. The militants were not appeased – they retreated to the mountains and fought a guerrilla war. The Russian heavy artillery had moved to the foothills, trying to get militants out of mountains.

In Chechnya, there were two bosses now. During the daylight, Russian troops controlled the country. Their numbers were vast, and they enjoyed the full might of the Red Army – airplanes, bombs, tanks, missiles, radar. Their dominance could hardly be challenged. And yet, when darkness came, the Chechen fighters crawled from their holes in the ground, and took up their weapons.

They owned the night, making sniper attacks on Russian patrols, firing rocket-propelled grenades at Russian positions, killing sentries silently in hand-to-hand combat, laying mines, sabotaging bridges and roads. They knew all the secret trails in the mountains where they were raised. They struck where they were least expected. They knocked helicopters from the sky; they destroyed entire troop convoys - small groups of men did this, most often on foot, moving stealthily and without a sound, dancing with death - their own and that of the Russians. Just before the sun rose, they would arrive in villages like this one, disappear into the cabins, and descend back down into the bowels of the Earth.

The Chechen people had long ago chosen the wolf as their symbol. To them, the wolf stands for independence and freedom. But the wolf has other meanings as well. The wolf is a nocturnal animal, and it hunts under cover of darkness. It is cunning, it is sly, and it is well-known to work the herd with senseless cruelty - wolves will slaughter all of the cattle in a field, consume what they can, then leave the rest to rot, a feast for the crows and the vultures. Wolves will murder like this again and again, until men with guns come and put a stop to it.

* * *

The darkness of the night came down, and Aslan appeared in a new military vest, an improved version made by his mother. It was the conventional military vest of Russian troops, that she perfected by sewing on a lot of pockets and added details. Now he could hold a lot more grenades and rounds on it – Aslan enthusiastically showed me the advantages of the vest in the soft light of the kerosene burner.

He spoke rapidly, in the excitement, describing to me his extraordinary waistcoat, as if to distract me from what was more important. We stood close to each other, considering all the convenient pockets for combat grenades.

He tried not to look me in the eye and his face was very serious in the dim lamplight. I already knew that he wanted to say something important.

Suddenly he stopped talking and picked up the lamp, lighting my face. His shining black eyes stared right into my own eyes, with their usual ability to drill down to my soul. But this time they were not cruel. He raised his other hand to my face, and held it against my cheek with a long touch. There was grief in his face.

"You will never go home."

My heart stopped beating.

"You are going on a mission."

The words sounded like a death sentence. I did not want to know anything about this mission. I was afraid to ask – I did not want to hear the answer. I would go insane with misery. The tears fell from my eyes. I couldn't hide them.

Aslan softly grabbed me by the neck and put my head on his shoulder. He hugged me with his hand and held me close. I was crying and could not stop. He patted me on the back, soothing me.

He whispered in my ear:

"I will come tomorrow, and we will figure out how to get you home."

He loosened his arms from me, and quietly left me alone.

But the next day he did not come. And for a few days after that, he also did not appear. I hadn't seen Mirza, either. Something had happened. Their sudden disappearance gave me a premonition of trouble - the feeling would not leave me.

Mission... mission? What did he mean? I had been thinking about it all the time since he left. I was panicking because of his absence.

He promised to help me. Tomorrow I may not be here anymore.

But now, knowing that he would help me, I could finally think how to implement a plan to escape. As soon as he reappeared, I would not waste any more time, and run away at the first opportunity – a suitably dark night.

Aslan will distract the fighters and leave the gate unlocked.

The gates need to be well lubricated – the scraping sound they make is loud and terrible. I will have to open the gates silently, and quietly get out of the house.

I'll have to go through the village quietly to no one else pays attention me. I need a dark handkerchief.

I need money to get out of the village on a passing car.

I could pretend to be deaf and dumb, and show a note to the driver that Aslan would write in advance.

When Aslan came, I would tell him about my plan and together we would work out the details.

I did not know what was going on behind the iron fence. He would tell me what to do. Maybe he would take me out of the village, by himself, and bring me closer to the Russian encampments.

Aslan was still the enemy, but he was also my only way out, my only friend. I knew that the war and his ideology were everything to him - a matter of honor. But I was sure that together we could come up with a suitable plan, and do it before I had to fulfill my mission, which I was afraid to ask about. I was sure he would not allow anything bad to happen to me.

I was sure that he had intense feelings about me. These long months had brought us closer together.

I waited for his return. I listened to all the sounds wafting through the door, trying to catch the hissing sound of his voice. I kept looking out the window. The creaking of the opening gates made me hold my breath, waiting to see his face.

I needed him.

Late at night, someone knocked on the door. Instantly, I woke up in alarm. The door was unlocked from the outside and there was the Shorty's mother in the doorway, holding the lantern, illuminating her face. She looked evil in the dim light. She stared at me, her eyes gleaming, her eyes shooting sparks, eyes that made me want to shrink away from her.

"You're leaving right now," she said. "Get up. You're being taken to another place."

I was still half asleep – I did not quite understand what she was talking about. She had a strong accent, but she was noticeably happy to say these words. I saw it and I felt it with the gooseflesh on my own skin. Aslan? He must be somewhere near.

"Where is Aslan? Is he here?"

"No more Aslan," she said. "He's gone! The Russians killed him!" *They killed him...*

My vision blacked out for a second. I nearly fainted from dizziness.

I was numb, in a stupor. I could not understand what I had to do at that moment.

I will be taken away? Where? No more Aslan?

No more Aslan...

I couldn't see anymore - my eyes dimmed with tears. With trembling hands, I began to quickly gather my simple belongings: everything that Aslan kindly brought me - toothpaste and toothbrush, a comb, wool knitted socks, and a small towel. I pulled a few remaining pads out from under the pillow, and a pair of spare underwear. I dropped all items into a square handkerchief, the one that Shorty's mother had given me. I put all the stuff in the center of it, and tied the edges to make a bag.

I sat on the edge of the bed, waiting.

He's dead... He's been killed...

No more Aslan.

I could not imagine it. I just could not believe it...

My life was over. I could not handle the death of Aslan – the tears did not stop for a minute. I mourned his death, along with all my dead hopes. He was a good person – in fact, the only one who reached out to me, as far as it was possible, and gave me a helping hand. My last chance for salvation had died with him.

I could no longer hope for anything. Aslan was my only defender, and he was going to get me out of captivity. He was about to help me. I needed just a few more days. The thought that my plan was slowly progressing gave me the strength to live on. Now I was lost. Everything that I had planned for so long and cherished had collapsed and turned into ashes. I was devastated – I didn't have the strength to look for a new way out. This was the end.

I couldn't take it anymore.

I was emaciated, and I was on the verge of insanity. It had been so long since I was captured and destroyed. I was no longer even sure if the life that I remembered, that I had before captivity, was really a true thing, and not just my dreams or a fiction. Maybe I had already gone insane, and I had never lived in a different world – all my life I was in captivity. This *is* my life.

I had reached the limit of my strength. In almost eight months, I had stayed strong. Up to this point.

I could not endure it any longer.

It had to stop.

CHAPTER SEVEN

May 1995
Valeroy, Chechnya

The trip was already too long. The off-roads, steep descents and ascents – the car was shaking like a rattle – and with it, everyone who was inside. The canvas top of the car was worn out, and air came through at the cracks. The roar of the wind and the motor were stunning. I was squeezed by the militants on both sides. Everything seemed to have jumped back in time several months, back to the night when I was taken away. There was the car, rushing on the road in the dark and I, alone in the whole world, surrounded by unfamiliar men. Only now I was sure that there was no way out and there was no hope. My spirit and my soul were weakened, and I could no longer resist the reality.

I can't take this anymore.

It has to stop.

Outside the window it was solid dark. We drove through the mountainous terrain, and I could not make out what was going on outside the window. No one spoke. The jeep roared - there was no sense speaking anyway. I had not seen any of these people before. They looked like ordinary militants – without age, with overgrown beards, dressed in dusty gray-black clothing, armed from head to toe. The machine guns were an integral part of their outfits, of their personalities, of their very beings.

I thought that the unbearable shaking would never end, but finally the car drove into a village and slowed down. Outside, in some places, there was a faint glimmer of light from the kerosene lamps. The night was impenetrable. Whoever was behind the wheel of the car knew this place inside out. The car stopped at a low built house with an open door. A kerosene burner on a table lit the insides of the house. I did not want to be pushed out, so I got out of the car myself, and stood in the dry dirt. It seemed like it was a remote mountain village, far from civilization. The air was filled with the coolness of spring, which filled the lungs and intoxicated with freshness.

There was no electricity here. It looked like there had never been electricity.

The dirt cracked unpleasantly under the thin soles of my pink fabric flats.

"Come on," one of my guards said.

A few seconds later, I heard the sound of more engines, and two other military vehicles drove up to the same house, illuminating all around with the light from their headlights. I heard men's voices – they were talking to each other in low voices.

I was ready to say goodbye to my life right then. I could run forward, into the darkness. Then they would hunt me, and shoot to kill. And everything would finally be over. Something held me back from doing this. *Not now.* I was not sure if they would actually kill me. I had to be sure that my attempt to end my life would be a hundred percent successful.

The house had one story, was very low and seemed quite large. I climbed the two steps to the porch and went inside through the open door, looking around. I was following the militant who was sitting to my left in the car. In the light of the kerosene lamp he looked overgrown and wild.

I quickly glanced at him just to see that he had a long beard. There was a handkerchief covering his head with an Arabic scarf. He seemed very tall, dressed in jeans and a T-shirt, and clad in army boots. He was wearing a military vest with lots of pockets, which were overfilled. His upper body bulged out so much from all the pockets, he seemed like he was encased in bubble wrap. He had an accent, but he spoke Russian cleanly. He carried a machine gun on his shoulder. It seemed that in the last few months I had only met these kinds of men. They were archetypes, they were stereotypes - each one a painted portrait of the Vainakh warrior.

In the light of the torch the house looked like a summer home. The large kitchen with the table pushed against the wall, and the kerosene lamp that lit up almost the entire room – it was all I saw. The rest was plunged into darkness.

Standing in the middle of a room filled with ominous dark light from the lamp, I had no idea what to do next. Grotesque shadows played on the walls – the man's in his vest inflated with grenade-filled pockets, and mine – they completed the picture of horror.

The man in the Arab scarf came close to me, and pointed somewhere ahead and to the floor. He indicated a hole in the floor, which had a trapdoor cover, and which was now thrown open. The hole was dark, as black as the night itself. I stared at the hole, the idea slowly sinking in – this pit was for me!

I was more pleased than disappointed or afraid – I wanted privacy. Any place would be better than to be among strangers ready to devour you at any moment.

The man lifted the kerosene torch from the table and escorted me to the door.

"Stay down there for right now."

The words "for right now" sounded like a threat. What did it actually mean? And what would come after?

"What if I need to go out to the bathroom?"

"Knock, and I'll open."

He crouched at the opening, lighting my way down to the cellar. A short staircase led from the top – it was only a few rungs down. In a long dress it was not very easy for me to climb down – the long skirt stuck between my legs.

The dungeon turned out to be a small pit, possibly designed for food storage. It was kind of chilly inside. My long woolen dress was helpful, and I had a pair of warm knitted socks with me. The cellar was about a man's height, depth and breadth. There was a stack of a few mattresses and a heap of different blankets and bedspreads on the floor making a bed. I stood inside the pit, shocked. The militant held the lamp aloft above me.

"Knock if you need to," he said.

Then he shut the coffin.

His massive boots made a loud sound on the wooden floor over my head. I was left standing in the pitch darkness, waiting for my eyes to adjust to the lack of light. Blind, I groped for the softness of the rugs on the bed and lay down, not covered.

The cellar was pleasantly cool. Stretching my legs, I suddenly realized that I was really tired. I was exhausted emotionally and physically. I had lost all my inner strength, I had no chance to escape, and I was almost buried alive in the ground. And it was not the end yet. I expected something worse and frightfully shocking – which would come for me very soon and would last until the end of my days. I could not let that happen. I choked back tears, but they rolled down my face, and I didn't even try to wipe them – I was lying motionless, cherishing one single thought in my mind – I can stop it.

I was no longer in agonizing fear – now I knew for sure that I could stop everything at any moment, if I only wanted to. I heard echoes of the men's voices in the distance, but I did not care…

I was awakened by the creaking wooden floor over my head. I barely opened my eyes – it was as if they were glued together with dried out tears. Just before I woke, I'd had a dream – I was hugging my mother. I tried to distract myself from the memory of my dream. I knew it would be heartbreaking. Above my head I spotted the lid that covered the entrance to the pit. It was made out of several wooden planks, nailed together. The rays of daylight lit through it. The dungeon was now very cold. I wrapped and covered myself with whatever was on the bed. The dress felt damp and unpleasantly chilled my whole body. The pit was not lighted enough even with the rays coming in. I had stayed in darkness most of the time for the past few months, so I think it would be fair if I would have developed the ability to see in total darkness, like a cat.

The cellar was just a pit, for the storage of food products. Now I was stored here. The air was heavy and cold – I felt buried alive. There was nothing else down here but a pile of the blankets.

Someone passed over head with a heavy tread. He came directly to the door and digging into the lock, opened the door, throwing it with a roar and a squeak on the wooden floor.

"You're still alive down there?"

His voice had a hint of mockery.

"You have to stay alive!"

He laughed at his own joke.

Above me the floors squeaked again – he walked away, leaving the lid open.

I did not want to go out. I would prefer to stay down here if I could. But despite my fright, it looked like I had to get out of the dungeon.

All that I was able to take with me from Gurchuloy were a few essentials, my only property, all of the things I had acquired with the help of Aslan – a toothbrush, toothpaste, underwear. I also had a small towel. I was glad that I already had everything I needed: I would not have to ask my jailers for anything.

I could barely climb out of the hole – I had no experience with such things and I had to learn it. The same guy who was here last night, the man in the Arab headscarf, was sitting on a chair in the corner. His feet in the huge boots rested on the chair opposite from him. Now his scarf was casually wrapped around his neck. His massive head was shaved.

In contrast, his beard seemed too long and stuck out crazily in different directions. The machine gun rested across his legs. He struck me as a thug, devoid of any human emotions whatsoever.

This one would kill, without regret – I could count on him.

The room was a square with one window in which there was no glass. A table and a few chairs – that's all that was happening here. The house seemed deserted, abandoned. The room led into a small hallway with two large windows covered with mesh. There was an aluminum hand-wash basin attached to the wall with a rusty sink underneath, and a bucket to drain the water. Against the wall there were a couple of pitchers.

Through the windows, covered by the mosquito net, the warm and fresh spring air was coming in. I washed my hands and face, brushed my teeth and filled the jug. Without inquiring about the whereabouts of the bathroom, I came out onto the porch to let the drops of water on my face dry. That moment, right in front of me, all of a sudden there opened a powerful and delightful view.

Even though I was depressed, I could not help but admire the natural beauty of this place. The village was surrounded by mountains. This house was located in the lower part of the village, right at the foot of the mountain. There were nothing but mountains all around. On the left, a little farther away, there was a forest climbing the slopes of the towering mountains behind it. Nature was so beautifully tranquil, despite the war, and I stared out at it with a fascinated gaze.

Even so, my condition did not match the natural beauty. I no longer wanted to be part of this world. I was ready to die.

I saw another pair of eyes watching me from the tent pitched out front. I probably looked stunned by the scenery – I hadn't seen anything like it in a long time. I was struck by the beauty and grandeur of the mountains. Everything here was fresh and delightful. It was by far the most beautiful morning in the past eight months. A warm breeze swept my hair over the shoulders. The insects were buzzing, the birds were chirping, the sounds of life were everywhere. Even so, it wasn't enough to convince me to stay.

Deep inside of me I could feel the dreary call of death - I did not want to be involved in this unjust world. I did not know how and when I would be able to stop it, but I had decided to give up - I was no longer going to fight for my life.

I heard a voice behind my back, like a shot.

"The bathroom is behind the house."

In front of the porch, in the yard, there was a spacious built-in seating area, like a gazebo, covered with a slate roof on one side. Inside, it was built fully of stone, as if it was hollowed out of the rocky mountainside. There was a massive table and stone benches covered with rags. There were some built-in ovens like the ones that I had seen in Gurchuloy. It was quite a large gazebo, and served as a good viewing platform for spying the area. Not knowing the path, I looked at the neighborhood all around, and slowly took a few steps behind the house. I immediately detected the clay structure of the bathroom, up on the hill.

Behind this house there were a few other houses built one above another, like a procession creeping up the mountain.

The path to the hill went through abandoned plant beds covered with weeds. The hillside was dry dirt, almost without any vegetation. The house and the yard were separated from other houses by a fence made of large steel mesh, which in some places was covered with wild climbing plants. The trees here were not much more than bushes.

The bathroom was a clay outhouse enclosing a hole dug in the ground. It was located on a wooden platform, and had a door made of long wooden planks. From the doorway, the outhouse overlooked the back of the house and the gazebo. Through the narrow gaps of the planks, it was easy to see what was going on inside the gazebo. I could also see into the house through the window that had no glass. I could make out the Arab scarf looming inside the house, and the barrel of a machine gun pointing straight up at me from the tent.

When I was done, I came back down the hill, into the house, and back down into the silent stillness of the dungeon.

* * *

I spent a week in the dungeon, except for a few forays into the world – to the bathroom and back, with the gunman accompanying me. Someone cared about my sustenance. In the morning, near the cellar on the table, I always found freshly baked bread, boiled eggs, or something else, wrapped in a clean towel. The food, especially the bread, was fresh and very tasty – the only thing I was glad about.

I did not want to go out into the fresh air at all. I just lay on the pile of blankets and stared blankly into the darkness. I mourned Aslan, my broken dreams and my pitiful life. I wanted to die right there, to end the suffering, and just leave the world unnoticed. I had to think and plan the way I would die, but I could not concentrate or come up with anything.

Being in captivity, with the passage of time, I discovered new sides of my character. In my past life, I had no idea that I could be a fighter, stand up for myself and not let circumstances break my spirit. For eight months I had fought my own war, all by myself. I'd had victories and defeats. Sometimes I did not even know where I found the strength to resist the onslaught. Now I just wanted to give up. I couldn't see any reason to continue to fight and stay optimistic and good spirited. I had tried my best to survive, and to stay hopeful. For what? To be sold into slavery? To be cut into pieces, my organs removed and sold into the illegal medical trade? Or God only knew what else. I was practically in my coffin already. I had to plan how to leave this world for good.

I was so young, and I had wanted so much to live! I wanted to laugh, to love, to embrace family and people who I adored. If I couldn't have my life back, I didn't want to stay alive.

As the days passed, and the more time I spent underground – virtually without moving – the more I sensed the approaching danger. Very soon, they would come for me. I did not know who "they" were, but I knew I wanted to be dead before they arrived.

The only plan I could come up with was to try my escape right in front of them, and make them shoot me in the back as I ran toward the mountains. There was no place to hide. The whole area was so open, they couldn't miss.

No one talked to me, and no one bothered me. It was as if they were waiting for someone or something. I liked being invisible, but I felt that it wouldn't last long. It was the calm before the inevitable storm.

The sounds that came from above – the men's voices, the car's engine, the squeak of the wood floors – everything I heard caused me anxiety, and made me regret that I had not realized my plan yet.

One morning, I woke up and needed to go upstairs. I climbed a couple of rungs on the ladder, and started to lift the lid, to give the loud sign that I needed to go out. The iron padlock banged hard against the steel loop at the top. After several minutes of banging like this, the wooden floors creaked and I heard a heavy tramp of military boots. A moment later the padlock was opened and the cover was thrown aside. Squatting at the entrance was a guy I had not seen before. I looked up at him from the depths of the pit.

"I want to come out."

He examined me closely with his dark eyes. He was dressed all in black – plain t-shirt with short sleeves, and pants tucked into battered army boots. He was young, though his thick black beard had abundant streaks of gray hair. His head was shaved. He was more handsome than unpleasant. Large dark eyes, with a nose that was slightly flattened, as though after a fracture. The broken nose didn't make him less attractive, but instead gave him a manly look.

He reminded me of Sergey, who also wore short hair. And his nose was broken, too, after several years of boxing. This Chechen reminded me of Sergey so much, that my heart shrank from all the sweet memories that came to my mind. They intruded from some other life, one that no longer seemed like mine.

I was carried away to those moments in happy times when we simply enjoyed each other, without noticing anyone around us. We did not care where we spent time – the main thing was that we were together. Each day, after I was done with my university classes, I could not wait to see him. We hung out in the cafes, went strolling in the park, or just sat around the house and chatted. Sergey was from a nice family, very polite young man. Older than me by two years, he had established his own business selling cars, and had successfully developed it. My mother adored him – his charming sense of humor could win anyone over. He looked after me beautifully and tenderly. We were both whimsical and explosive. If we happened to quarrel over trifles, we did it vigorously and passionately, but then we immediately made up with even greater passion.

The man who opened the lid of my dungeon didn't have the same tender feelings towards me. He just watched my actions as if I was a monkey at the zoo, and enjoyed his power over me.

On both sides of his body, there were two holsters where pistols dangled. It was strange to see someone without a machine gun. He did not seem ordinary village boy – he was well-kept and tidy. Maybe he was a mercenary?

"Do you mind if I come out? I need to use the bathroom."

After a long pause, I repeated my question again.

"Crawl out!" he said. He spoke cheerfully and without an accent.

He spoke in such a friendly way, it was as if we had known each other for a hundred years. He was definitely not local. I awkwardly walked up the stairs and sat down on the edge of the wood floor, legs still hanging into the hole. My handkerchief was resting on my shoulders. I always wore it on my shoulders, so that it was always with me, and I could cover my hair if I needed to. I felt more comfortable having my hair covered. I drew less attention – my hair grew down below my shoulders, and its blonde color was way too light compared to the dark hair of the Chechens. I put the handkerchief on and stood up to my full height. Spring was here. The air got warmer every day. It was so nice to feel the fresh air after a heavy night underground.

I went into the narrow hallway towards the sink. I brushed my teeth and washed my face with cold water. I filled the jug and went out. The new guard – because of his shaven head I thought of him as "Sheared" – followed behind me. Nothing had changed, except for the guards. And maybe the guards weren't even new. Lately I had been in a coma – just today I seemed to be getting my senses and vision back. As I climbed to the outhouse, I heard men's voices talking somewhere nearby.

Upon returning, I stayed in front of the porch for a second. A strange thought occurred to me.

"Do you mind if I sit here for a bit?" I said.

He thought for a moment. He shrugged.

"No."

He went to the gazebo and sat down on the bench without taking his eyes off me.

I sat on the wooden porch in front of him, and breathed deeply – I could not get enough of the fresh morning air. It was warm and it was beautiful. On the left, a bit further, on the hill, right before the forest, I could see a neighbor's house, white with the same reddish roof and mesh fence surrounding it. All kinds of sounds filled the earth in this hour of the morning. The murmur of a mountain stream, the play of birdsong and crackling of insects were coming from somewhere. I was surrounded by the mountains on all sides. It seemed that I was on the edge of the earth.

What is behind these mountains?

What if I run now?

Where?

Over the fence?

Jump over the fence in this long dress?

Which direction do I run after that?

Thousands of questions flooded my mind, and I couldn't give a precise answer to any one of them. What would happen to me if I got caught instead of being killed?

From the house next door, a woman came out, stopped at the fence and looked straight at me. What did she know about me? What would happen if I asked her for help? Sheared did not seem worried that that woman saw me.

What was wrong with these people? Did their beliefs allow and encourage them to deprive an innocent human of her freedom?

The woman wore a long dress and a tied Chechen scarf around her head. She continued to stare at me. There seemed to be pain in her eyes. Or maybe, I just thought that and my mind was playing tricks on me. I was too far away to see the feeling in the eyes of a complete stranger.

A group of men came out of the house behind her. I did not linger on the porch, so as not to draw attention to myself. I went back inside. Bread was waiting for me on the table. I climbed down into the pit, and Sheared cranked the key in the lock.

In the evening, I went out again for a quick bathroom visit. Sheared was still there. My heart sank when I saw a group of militants under a canopy. They were talking. Upon my appearance, they seemed to start talking about me. A wave of fear passed through me as I walked uphill – the feeling of impending disaster.

The sun had set. The thought of new painful experiences in the near future, perhaps more terrible than before, caused me an internal conflict. I struggled with myself. Was it worth to me, right now, to jump out of the bathroom and run, hoping that they would shoot and kill me? My suffering would end immediately. But what if they didn't kill me right away, and only hurt me? Then my suffering would start in the worse way – I would be dying in torture, slowly bleeding in agonizing pain. But I could no longer stand the life imposed upon me, either.

Oh, God, why was this so hard?

To plan your own death is not easy, especially if you don't really want to die.

I had always made choices as I was advised by my inner voice and intuition. Once again, it told me to skip this battle. I did not run away – it was a stupid plan. I had to do something that would give me predictable results.

The stars in the sky began to light up one after the other. Their distant beauty moved something inside me. Suddenly I wanted to stay here for a second, and look at the starry night.

Before I descended back to the cellar, I asked:

"Can I stay by the window for a minute?"

He was not an asshole, this guy. It was clear from the start, when I saw him the first time. He looked like Sergey, so he couldn't be a bastard. Now it was confirmed.

"Okay," he said.

He sat on the floor near the wall and began to light up the kerosene lamp in the impending dusk. I stood next to the window, where there was no glass. The pleasant night's coolness had replaced the day's hotness. I stood in the darkness, turned my back on the guy, exposing my chest and face to the stars, which were slowly popping alight, here and there. It felt so incredibly wonderful to be in the dark, under the starry sky, which had no end. What a pity that I had to leave this world and without even a chance to understand why I was born.

I felt euphoric. There was no single human sound now. The moist spring air filled my lungs, intoxicated, and carried away to some unfamiliar reality. This night on Earth struck me and filled me with joy. The tranquility was only broken by the pleasant sounds of the night. I could hear the mountain river flowing, cascading downhill, somewhere far away. The night birds called. I wanted to soar high into the sky, all the way to the stars, and fly away from here, home. To my mom. I looked at the dark and starry sky with my eyes wide open and thought that somewhere, she might also be looking at the same sky, and see the same stars, and pray to God for me to be returned home.

Mama! Suddenly, it was clear to me. How could I dare to think of dying? I couldn't do that to her! I would not lose hope. I would not lose faith. I would find a way to escape, not to get myself killed, but only to get home. Silent tears of sudden illumination flowed down my face. It was if scales had fallen from my eyes, and only now could I see clearly. I had just realized a new way to get out of the captivity.

That night I did not sleep at all, struck by this new idea. All new strength had come to me from somewhere above. I felt that I had made another victory over my own self.

I needed to escape, but in a way where they wouldn't notice me or shoot me. It was almost impossible to do, but I had to find a way.

All night I pondered the options, but none of them seemed like they would work.

Now I had to find a way to be outside as much as possible.

Every morning and evening, going to the bathroom, I quietly watched what was going on around me. I had only a few minutes to scout out everything carefully.

At least two militants were always there when I was out. One of them was always close and near. In the evening, from down in the pit, I heard men's voices and the sound of cars departing. Early in the morning the sound of men's voices resumed. The militants were hiding in the mountain villages by day, and conducting their brutal guerrilla war in the night. Most likely, this village was one of their hideouts.

Often, from the porch, I noticed the neighbor woman. Our eyes always met. The neighbor, it seemed, was either always there or would come out and wait for my arrival.

The neighbor woman was watching me, and I did not know if it was pity or hatred. In those rare moments when I was able to stay on the porch, longer, I could see a group of militants leaving her house. Perhaps she was cooking for them, and one of them was her son or a husband. She had three young sons, about eight to ten years old. They became frozen at the fence, with their mouths open, when they saw me.

* * *

One morning, on the way to the bathroom, I suddenly heard the neighbor woman's voice. She spoke to my guard over the fence. I never heard her speak before. On the way back from the bathroom, the guard told me something that put me in a real shock:

"She's calling you to her house to have breakfast."

I could not believe my ears. I was ready for anything, but not for a manifestation of human kindness. I almost imagined it was some kind of trick.

Over the past eight months, I had been on a long journey, one where I had to deal with many different people. It was as though, when you least expected, the good people would appear from nowhere. Was it God's work? I didn't know.

The Chechen people – they had appeared in my life out of nowhere as if they were materialized from a parallel world – one which I did not know about until I woke up in a dark car on that fateful night. New faces appeared and completely filled the space around me, trying to force out the memories of my past life and everything that was dear to me. People kept entering my life, and it scared me. I did not know what they would bring – new pain or salvation. I wanted to see the goodness and compassion in each one, imagining the fairytale with the happy ending. But each time, this dream was broken on the rocks of reality.

People who seemed good at first glance could later turn into the cold-blooded monsters. They also could remain good, but up to a certain limit. I had met a few good people here, but they could not help me. Despite that, I still wanted to believe that there were no good or bad nations. Cruelty and kindness can take place in any of them.

The guard escorted me to the woman's house, and we stopped at a summer kitchen under a canopy, with a large table covered with a tablecloth. The stove was lit with coals, and in a frying pan there was something that smelled delicious. I had smelled the woman's cooking a few times before in the air – each time, in my imagination, it brought me home.

The guard sat nearby. The neighbor did not say a word and I did not speak either, but somehow I felt her good intentions and the warmth of her heart. I realized that she knew everything about me – I could read it in her eyes. A woman without age, in a long dress and a scarf, tied around her head, she looked like a typical Chechen woman, who never knows fatigue or rest. She fed her men, and now it was time for the women to have food. I have learned that in Chechnya, the men and women are not supposed to sit at the table at the same time.

She looked at me with pity in her dark and tired eyes, just like when I saw her on the porch for the very first time. And I was not wrong then – even from the distance I could see the true compassion. She stared at me, gesturing, kindly pointing me to a chair. I thanked her and sat down. She brought a hot skillet full of fried eggs sprinkled with cottage cheese.

The taste of the food was amazing, and I enjoyed every bite of it. She brought out hot, freshly baked bread – the same as I found every day on the table near the pit. I wanted to cry from her kindness. She just sat at the opposite side of the table, did not eat anything, and stared at me. I could not read her mind, but in her eyes I saw something deeper than even compassion or pain. I was so grateful and I was sure she could read it on my face. I did not want to leave her home – it was something peaceful and hopeful, something that I missed so much.

That night, in the dark, a realization came:

She knows what the future holds for me.

That would explain her compassion. Even so, I could not wait for her to call me again.

Time went on, and I could not find a way out. The more time passed, the less time was left to escape. I felt the approach of something terrible right around the corner. The gunmen were waiting for something. None of them were familiar to me – I had seen none before in the previous places. They were a completely different group.

I wondered what kept them from hurting me. It seemed to me that I had been sold, perhaps into slavery, and they were waiting for a convenient time to ferry me to my new owner. Nothing else seemed to make sense. Clearly, they didn't intend for me to live here underground the rest of my life.

The thoughts made me paranoid. Each creaking floorboard above my head terrified me. I had horrible dreams. I constantly dreamt about my mother. I did not know whether she was still alive and healthy. The dreams shattered my sleep, and I would awaken in tears. My mom and I were both crying in my dreams – tears of grief and sorrow mostly, but sometimes tears of joy.

It was impossible to get out. Armed bandits kept an eye on me at all times. The only chance for escape was my trips to the bathroom. I examined the structure made of clay for a few days. The roof was too high – I could not jump that high to try to get through it. Without a ladder or chair, it was impossible for me to reach it.

A few days later, the neighbor called me again. By now, I had realized that my regular guard was her husband, or brother. That was how she was able to persuade him to let me come over. He was a big guy – one of those who brought me here from Gurchuloy. He wore his Arabic scarf all the time. He looked ageless and threatening, and sounded bossy and loud. The second militant stayed at the gazebo, and I was guarded just by the Scarf guy.

My second visit, she kept me at her house much longer. She spoke a little Russian, although with great difficulty. She spoke a single phrase at a time, but I understood her perfectly.

"My name is Laila."

I tried to thank her for her kindness and tell her how delicious her food was. I was not sure how much she understood. She smiled back at me, and that was enough. I wanted to scream for help, to throw myself at her feet and beg her to help me escape. But I couldn't kill my chances - she was one of them, even though a very kind one. She probably couldn't help me anyway. This was a war – a war of her children, a war of her country. What would happen to her if she tried to help me? I couldn't let her suffer because of me.

The front was slowly moving towards us. I guessed that the Russians wanted to lure the Chechen fighters from their mountain shelters. Would they kill civilians? Since Aslan had died, I didn't know anything about the war.

In the pit, sometimes I could hear some strange sounds. I did not know what it was at first, but right away this distant muffled thunder terrified me. It made my heart sink from a sense of helplessness. The sounds were flat, faraway and lifeless, like someone randomly beating a heavy African drum in the distance. I almost couldn't hear them at all. I did not fully understand what was happening. I had not seen the bombing up close and could not identify it by ear. But gradually I realized, and then I knew: what else could it be? It was a voice of War.

I could not help but focus all my attention on them. Everything else ceased to exist. Only the sounds, like sinister musical instruments – mystical drums - untuned, dull. They promised nothing but horror and pain. Even later, when the beating stopped and a dead ringing silence covered the earth, the far-sounding drums remained in my memory like an obnoxious and evil symphony – a constant reminder of my youth that was taken away, and the deprivation of the right to live, the right to love.

I did not want to believe that there was no way to escape, but a new problem had arisen as the bombing came closer. If I wasn't killed by the militants, there was a good chance I would be killed accidentally by the Russians. I had to send a message to the Russian troops and let them know I was here. But how to do that?

May 1995
Astrakhan, Russia

It had been almost eight months. The woman avoided family and friends. She hated them because they could live without her. Friends did not call so often anymore, and were not interested in the latest news about her daughter. There was no more news anyway. Everyone got used to the fact that she was gone. All of them, except her. She refused to accept her daughter's absence. Even if a hundred years passed, she would wait for her child and she would hope for her return.

The police formally continued to search for her daughter in Chechnya, hoping that someone would accidentally discover the place of her confinement and inform the Russian troops if she was still alive. They could do no more than this. Chechnya was a bloody mess. Against a backdrop of mass killings and the disappearance of hundreds of people, the chance of finding one missing person was reduced to zero.

Was she alive? Only God knew. The woman begged Him to give her a sign. She prayed for hours, to oblivion, to blackouts, begging God to bring her back. Since mid-February she had not received any phone calls from the terrorists. They were gone, and the connecting thread was gone with them.

She prayed, she believed, and she received a sign. The sign came in the form of an elderly woman, one of the parishioners in the church, with the beautiful name Taya – she unexpectedly came up to the woman and stared into her eyes. Seemed like Taya could read the inner pain and anguish in her eyes.

"What happened, child?"

The woman began the story – she had told it many times, but this time felt different.

"My daughter had been taken."

Taya listened to the tale. At the end, she gave the woman nine church candles.

"Light up one of them every night and let it finish," she said. "Believe and hope. She will come back. Do not let hope die."

When no hope remains, a person will cling to any thread, even if it is incredibly thin, in order to go on living – so the woman believed Taya.

Later, the woman grew impatient for the night to come, so she could light the first candle. She sat next to the candle in the dark, watching it cast long dancing shadows on the wall. She sat with it until it burned down completely, and the entire time, her eyes did not shed a single tear. There was something mysterious and attractive in that flickering light.

Was Taya a witch, or a shaman? It did not matter – the task she had given the woman inspired strength and hope.

Each new morning, she could hardly wait for the night to come. This magic ceremony was going to be the answer; it would bring her daughter back. She found herself investing all of her faith into it. She would sit next to burning candle and gaze out the window, and she would feel in her heart that the day was approaching – her beloved daughter felt closer as every moment passed.

Then she was down to only one, the ninth and last candle. She lit it in awe and terror. She believed in omens and in the signs she was receiving – her whole present world was concentrated in this last candle and it could hopelessly collapse.

Days had passed since she watched the last one burn down, and nothing had changed. Despair began to conquer her fading hope.

Every night, when she could not fall asleep, the woman drew the heavy curtains wide open and looked out the window. She turned her eyes up the sky and cried out to God. Looking to the distant, endless dark space, she was overcome by a feeling – it seemed that somewhere far away, her lonely daughter was looking at the same stars and thinking about her.

June 1995
Valeroy, Chechnya

I waited for Laila's invitation every morning. I hoped she would call me again, but she did not, and I had not seen her in a while. Her tall and scary relative hadn't shown up either. Every morning and evening, I jumped out of the pit and hurried outside, trying to find Laila, searching with my eyes scanning all around. Finally, some days later, she reappeared, standing at the fence. She waved me over.

Soon, I was once again in her home having late breakfast. Being there made me happy and grateful. It gave me a sense of normalcy that had long been missing from my life. We were neighbors, she and I, only she lived in this pretty, open, wood-framed home, and I lived in a dark pit underground. But she didn't treat me as a prisoner – she treated me as her guest. It was a beautiful feeling, a civilized feeling, to be a guest in someone's home.

If only I could do something for her. I noticed a pile of undone dishes – left after the whole group of militants had eaten, I guessed. For a long time, I had been missing everyday trifles – simple small home chores. There was a large basin of water on a big boulder prepared for washing. And I said:

"May I wash them?"

Her little sons were spinning around behind the fence. The guard seemed to have dozed off under the canopy. Laila nodded in agreement, and then quickly came up to me, took something from her apron pocket, and quickly hung it around my neck. I jumped back in surprise, but then I saw that it was a delicate lace string, with a tiny, stitched, brown leather bag hanging from it.

"Wear it," she whispered. "It will help you."

I quickly hid the tiny pendant under my dress collar. We washed the dishes in silence, and I could not stop thinking about this leather pouch.

What was in it?

* * *

Lately, I slept very little. In those short oblivion moments when I drifted off, I had dreams about my mother – again and again – every night. Then I woke up in the dark, choking back tears, in desperation.

That one morning before sunrise, I heard footsteps right over my head. I really wanted to go upstairs – I didn't know what time it was and whether someone would open the door for me at such early hour. I went up on the ladder and knocked on the lid. The door lifted a tiny bit, making the loud sound of the iron lock hitting against the loop. Someone was in the house in the vicinity of the cellar. The lid soon was lifted and I saw Laila's relative. I was delighted and hopeful – his presence was always a chance I could go to her house. It was too early for breakfast – the sun had just begun to rise, weak sunlight peaking from the horizon behind the mountains.

I was hurrying up the hill with the guard at my back when I noticed Laila in the yard near her house. I wanted to let her know that I was also up, in the hope that she would invite me to her home earlier than usual. I hid inside the outhouse. Everything seemed different in the twilight. It was still dark, and the guard was waiting at the fence. The sound of arriving cars cut the morning silence. Through the gaps between the wooden planks of the toilet door, I saw two military cars stopped out front, green with canvas roofs. Despite the darkness, the headlights were off. A few men disembarked from the cars and dispersed. The militants had returned from a night operation and had gone into their shelters to rest.

I would like to see Laila. She noticed me on the porch, and nodded to me. In the darkness, I looked right into her eyes.

"Laila, can I help with the housework?"

I shuddered as I asked, quite sure that my request would be denied.

The sleepy guard dropped a few words with Laila. Unfortunately, I still could not understand their language. I knew a few words of Chechen that Aslan taught me, but mostly I sensed the language by the tone of the voices. Laila spoke slowly and persuasively, almost hypnotically. The scarf guy, on the contrary, had an intimidating low voice, and spoke fast. But she knew how to convince him.

I had been here, under their supervision, for about a month – the whole time, I had showed myself as very quiet, scared and broken – I did not need to pretend it. The captors grew accustomed to seeing me helpless and pathetic. Recently my inner state has changed, and I would like them to continue thinking that I was still miserable and weak. I wanted to show them I was well and truly beaten – I was helpless, I was impotent. I need to finally put their vigilance to sleep. The guard's supervision began to weaken. The militants had more on their minds than me – their thoughts were filled with war and blood, and possibly, with the very real prospect of their own impending deaths. They still watched me, but the effort was already less careful, less close, with eyes that were less suspicious – it seemed like they were just going through the motions.

Today I was in the backyard of Laila's home. I was like a balloon drifting out of their sight. I had never been so far away from my underground pit and from the guard tasked with watching me. It felt amazing, like a breath of freedom. There were farmyard hens and a barn in the back. The yard reached to the cliff, with a low mountain creek running through it. I had not seen it before, but had always heard its peaceful murmur. We were surrounded by towering mountains. To the left of her house, a forest climbed deep into the space between them. The small village, just a few houses, seemed perfectly hidden down here.

Laila's house was the closest to the woods, separated from it by a low fence. I kept glancing at the forest, trying not to stare. It was dense, almost black, an army of trees standing close together like a wall, a dark and foreboding forest from a medieval children's tale – Hansel and Gretel could disappear into such a forest.

Perhaps I could as well.

Half of the barn had been converted into a garage where one of the jeeps was kept. A lonely cow grazed near the house, right next to the forest belt. The spirit of freedom intoxicated me. Having appeared suddenly in this new territory, the thought pierced me:

Run! Right now!

I wouldn't make it across the mountain stream unnoticed. But the forest – if I reached it I would disappear. The feelings electrified me – I had only to wait for the guard to be absent for a moment or for a lapse in his attention.

I turned to Laila.

"What can I help you with?" I said.

I was going to go for it. I was a hundred percent sure. The idea made me feverish with excitement and thrill. Seeing me busy with household chores, helping Laila, I had hoped that the Scarf would weaken his attention for a second. Laila's three young sons played nearby. The sun was rising, and the day was promising to be beautiful and warm.

Two ideas were at war in my mind. One very simple thought: *Run!*

And a much more complicated jumble – a plague of questions and fears, which made clear the absurdity of the first idea.

Laila distracted me from my inner struggle. She handed me an empty bucket and gestured at the cow in the field.

"Milk," she said.

A moment later, I was standing about fifteen feet from the animal with the empty bucket in my hand. This was the closest I had ever been to a cow. Previously, I had seen cows from afar, and they always seemed like quiet and calm creatures, peacefully grazing the fields, slowly chewing the grass, carelessly looking around.

My grandmother had a small farm, which consisted of a single huge pig named Borka. I was young then and never approached the pig closer than ten feet. I was not allowed to go any closer. Then something bad happened to Borka – the thing that was supposed to happen, and the reason he was there from the beginning. I was very sorry for the huge hog. I cried when I learned that he was no longer with us.

I slowly approached the cow with a bucket and noticed her nostrils, which seemed to flare like the nostrils of a bull in bullfight somewhere in Spain. She looked straight at me. It seemed that in a second she would start to beat a hoof on the ground and rush to attack me. She appeared to read my mind, and knew what I was thinking about. She definitely felt my fear.

Many times in the movies and cartoons I had seen how easily the farm people milked the cows. It was only necessary to approach her confidently and begin to pull the udder. They say that animals know when someone is afraid of them, and then they begin to feel superior. I could not let that happen. I walked quickly up to the cow. I pet her back to show that I was the boss here, letting her know that everything was fine and calm, and letting her know that she was about to be milked. She was just peacefully standing there, chewing slowly whatever she had in her mouth, lulling me into a false sense of security. She showed me that she agreed to our new relationship. My heart started melting at how cute she was, when all of a sudden, she shook her long tail like a whip in my direction. It was very unexpected. Any sudden movement, at a time when you're already so alert, immediately stimulates the instinct to flee. I screamed and jumped back five steps, dropping the bucket on the ground.

Someone burst out in laughter behind me. I turned and there was Laila. The cow seemed totally careless. She kept moving her tail around, just fighting off the annoying flies around her butt. I burst out laughing too. Laila confidently took the bucket from the ground, squatted down on her haunches and began to quickly and nimbly milk the cow, showing me how to do it. The cow seemed calm and happy.

I sat down close to Laila and tried to pull the cow's udder, squeezing warm milk in the bucket. It drizzled in different directions, everywhere but the bucket, but I was not appeased. After some time I got the hang of it and the task was accomplished. I was covered with splashes of milk, but the bucket was almost full.

This short but funny episode made me forget about my intention for a few moments. Laila was a good mother, a good person and I was very grateful to her. But I wanted to go home, and be among the people that I loved. There, where I belong.

Trembling with excitement, I decided to run right now, contrary to my cowardly inner voice. I filled a pitcher with water and stepped closer to the fence, to clean my hands and dress. I had never been so close to the forest and to my dream. I tried to drown out my inner voice, which was screaming NO!

Adrenaline overwhelmed me: I had never been so close to the goal. This was my chance.

Uncontrollable excitement evolved my whole being. Everything around me took on a surreal cast. I could hear my own heart beating – super slow and extremely loud. I could hear the sound of insects tunneling in the ground, and the world seemed to move in slow motion, growing slower and slower all the time. I washed my hands as centuries passed – nearby, the trees in the forest swayed in the breeze, moving with the same infinite slowness of the snails crawling on their trunks.

I watched what was happening, searching for the smallest details, looking for the one piece of evidence that would say to me, clearly and without doubt:

RUN!

RUN NOW!

Laila's little boys were playing near the guard and the vehicle. The Scarf did not seem to pay any attention to us. I was pretending to carefully clean my dress of the milk splashes. Laila put the satisfied cow into the barn, then picked up the bucket of milk and headed toward the shed with it. My heart pounded furiously. I was ready to make my move. My brain was on fire, the synapses twitching and sizzling.

But then something changed. An ominous silence suddenly descended. It came from everywhere and descended upon me, fully covering me like a heavy blanket, like invisible hands pressing against my ears from both sides. It was as if, for a split second, every sound in nature had stopped, including my own heartbeat. You could feel the fear and anxiety deep inside you - something powerful and deadly was just about to begin. In the deep grass, the crickets were not chirping. The sheep had stopped bleating. The cows were quiet. No small birds called from the trees, and no great hawks cried out from the sky. Nature herself was paralyzed in terror.

Then there was a hissing whistle – its shriek so loud that it penetrated like knives through my ears and shattered my brain.

It struck fear into me that I would never forget. If you ever hear that sound, you will remember it for the rest of your days. Everything happened fast, but seemed to take a long time. There was a sudden flash and explosion somewhere very close, in the forest. Under my feet, the earth did not merely tremble – the very ground was lifted up and then put back down by the blast.

The Russians were attacking.

I saw Laila, her eyes wide, her young face a mask of horror. She dropped the bucket, rushing to pick up her screaming children. The white stream of the milk poured onto the ground and down the hill. I did not run toward the burning woods. I ran for my own hole in the ground, my dungeon.

The war was here. It had arrived for me at last.

My breath came in horrible shredding gasps. I ran faster than I ever had before. I could feel the shells screamed down from the mountains above us towards the forest bringing an apocalyptic rain of fire. The ground groaned and shuddered, rising and falling, cracking apart in an earthquake manufactured and delivered by man.

I burst through the house.

I crouched, and scrabbled for the trapdoor to my pit. What good would it do? A single bomb would splinter this house into ten thousand matchsticks, and leave a crater three stories deep.

I could not think about it, I dropped into the hole, then yanked the cover down on top. I lay in the dark, covering my ears with my hands, screaming to match the sounds of the bombs, screaming though I could not even hear myself. Outside and above me, the sky roared. Here, under the Earth, the ground shook with each new hit.

I had spent months afraid, but had never experienced fear to match this... pure terror. It was crystalline, perfect, like a diamond. There could be nothing like this state of mind. No thought, no feeling, no past, no future, no longing, no planning, no choices to make. Nothing I could do would change the outcome – the bombs would land on me, or they wouldn't.

Sometime later, the quiet returned. The bombing had stopped. Only then could I begin to think again. The Russian troops were so close. My salvation was just a cannon shot away.

Was anyone else in the village alive?

The dungeon was not locked. The fear was overwhelming. I could get out if I wanted and somehow let the Russian troops know about my existence. Or I could be immediately killed as soon as I showed myself. In movies, I had seen the survivors spread letters on the shore hoping to be noticed by a passing airplane. HELP! It would be virtually impossible to implement. How could I put a long word of seven letters:

ПОМОГИТЕ

on the ground? Only in one case, and that was if everyone else in the village was dead. As much as I wanted to escape, I would never wish for such an outcome for Laila's family.

Soon, everything came back to life again. In the house, people began to stir. I was not alone. Lingering fear from the explosions overpowered any other feelings. I remained sitting in the shelter, barefoot, my hands clasped, begging to something – God, Allah, the spirits of the Chechen ancestors who walked these mountains for all eternity – for an end to the war.

At dusk, I climbed out of the dungeon – Laila came to see me. I was very surprised and touched. She brought me my pink flats, which I had lost after the bombing started. Fortunately, all her children were alive. We hugged and she told me she was going to stay with some relatives in their home in another village, with her children, for a while. I could not hold back the tears – I would be left alone again. I could not believe that this woman, who was so kind to me, was leaving.

Laila brought me a lot of food, carefully wrapped in a linen towel. Her husband was taking them to a safer place. Finally, I knew that the Scarf was her husband. She spoke to me in broken Russian. She told me that the bombing would continue. Over the hill, on the right, there were Russian troops positioned to eradicate militants from the mountains. She was sorry to leave me. We survived the bombing together and we stayed alive. We felt incredibly close.

That evening, they left. Laila was gone. The Scarf was gone too. I was locked in the pit.

The next day, I sat in the dungeon all day, praying for the end of the war. In the afternoon, the shelling resumed – somewhere near – the deaden and monotonous sounds of explosions filled my tiny underground shelter. I was again falling into despair. The darkness around me was inexorably condensing.

I was in the middle of the war by accident. I was not on anyone's side – and could not accept either one. I was fighting my own war for survival, in the midst of someone else's war. I was Russian and I was deeply sorry for the Russian soldiers who were in the war on the orders of people who would never see the fighting. In Russia, the soldiers were as expendable as live ammunition. One shot, and cast aside as junk. The Chechen fighters – they had been boys only yesterday, who believed in their ideology, and went to be killed to defend their country. In Chechnya, where the value of death had been steadily growing, everything was decided by the politicians, and by the leaders of the clans. Their independence was so important to them that the entire nation could die preserving it.

I just wanted peace – for everyone.

And I wanted to go home.

June 7, 1995
Valeroy, Chechnya

Lately, I often had two similar dreams, with different meanings. Every time in these dreams there were the both of us – my mother and me. In the first one, we were standing on the opposite sides of a long bridge, each surrounded by a small number of people. We were separated by the bridge and looked across at each other standing as if we were frozen. We could not run to each other, as if some powerful force paralyzed us and pinned to the ground and would not let us budge. We could not even cry out to each other – our faces were petrified. We only could see each other in the distance, and I saw that the tears were dropping from my mother's eyes, full of pain and despair. And I was crying as well. I remember that a strong wind blew away our tears immediately, so that they were invisible to the people around us. The wind was violent, and the tears dried out instantly. So we stood facing each other, helpless and heartbroken.

The second dream, on the contrary, was kind and warm. It was my mom and I, and we were just hugging each other without saying any words, like after a long separation, and we wept tears of joy. We could not be more happy.

After these dreams, I usually woke up sobbing – sometimes my eyes were nearly glued shut from the dried tears. Even after I awoke, I felt heartache the rest of the day. Sometimes, right after I woke up, I could still physically feel the remnants of warmth from the touching and hugs.

On this day, I felt that something had awakened me. Opening my eyes, I could not remember my dreams, but I could still feel the heat remaining from someone's touch on my shoulder. I felt this distinctly – something had touched me on the shoulder and woken me up. My eyes were wide open – I was full of energy. I felt the high humidity in the pit this morning, inhaling it with my nostrils. Normally, on awakening, I could determine if it was morning or night by the strips of weak light, filtering through the loose planks above my head. This time, it was really dark – the sun had not yet thought to rise.

I felt the desire to go outside, and it was not my usual morning desire to get out of the cave and go to the bathroom. My handkerchief hanging as a pioneer tie on the shoulders, had grown damp and unpleasant after the night underground. My woolen blue dress felt cold and heavy. I slid out from under the pile of blankets. In the dark, I found my canvas slippers and put them on. There was not much left of them – they were now worn-out flops with their backs hammered to the soles, torn at the seams. I groped for the ladder. Keeping one hand on the ladder's step, I raised my hand in the familiar gesture to knock on the lid of my tomb. Surprisingly, my fist lifted the wooden square of the loose cellar door, making it clear that the door was not locked from the outside.

That was strange. Last night, I had heard the painfully familiar sound of a key turning in the lock. No one had moved above my head since then.

I climbed another step up and lifted the door of the cellar. The metal loop was loose and free. It took a little effort to get out of the dungeon. I had never come out like this, as one of the captors always unlocked the door and threw it back. The door was not heavy, just thin wooden boards, fastened together – it was not that difficult to raise it. I climbed out and sat on the wooden floor looking around. It was not very dark out. The twilight time. The hinge lock had been placed on the floor. Outside the windows, covered with mosquito nets, there was dead silence. It was unusual not to see a single living being and not to hear a single sound. More than unusual – it was happening for the first time.

For a moment I thought that the bombing would start in a second. Nature seemed frozen in silence. Like the last time, for a fraction of a second just before the shelling started, as if the earth was getting ready to take the pain. The birds stopped singing, no insects made a sound, the wind stopped howling – everything froze for half of a moment.

The silence was piercing – like in one of those moments, except, this time the silence lasted much longer than usual. No explosions followed. And still there was no one around. I felt as if I was the only survivor on the planet after a nuclear explosion. Night was turning into dawn slowly. I stood up to my full height, walked over to the sink, and grabbed an empty vessel, trying to figure out what was going on. I did not need to go to the bathroom. Not knowing why I did it, I slowly poured water into the pitcher. There was not a single creature around.

Through the sheer mesh I observed the great darkness of the sky and slowly approaching dawn. It was so strange. Also, my feelings were strange. I felt like I was that same endless sky – I had been filled with some hitherto unknown sixth sense. Just like a new day was born inside that huge sky, and a great sun was slowly rising, I had a new feeling inside of me that grew into a stunning and powerful *thought*. The *thought* inside my head was growing and developing with the greatest speed, illuminating my mind as the rising sun lights up everything around it. I shuddered when I realized and understood what kind of *thought* it was.

I no longer felt the same.

I went out towards the bathroom, passing the weeds, through the ranks of the wild growing plants, up the hill, with the pitcher in my hand. There was no one but me. Where were all the militants who should return with the dawn? Where were the guards? Who had opened the lock?

My new *thought* reached the top of my head and was now screaming in my mind:

THIS IS YOUR CHANCE.

It was the moment I had been waiting for the whole long eight months, that I had planned a hundred times in my dreams, *this was it.* Although this did not look like any of the escapes from my imagination, I knew for sure - *this was it.*

The earth was waking up, the sun had not yet appeared, but its rays had already touched the sky as if it was coming up from out of the ground, as if it lived under the ground, as I did. I went into the bathroom, and looked around, through the narrow slits between the planks, and even then I did not see any movement. I could not lose a second. I quickly went outside, leaving the pitcher on the bathroom floor.

Then I walked away.

I walked towards where all the recent shellings had come from. To the mountains. Adrenaline was about to explode inside of my body, and my heart wanted to jump out of my chest. I kept going forward. I forced myself not to turn around. I was afraid to turn and see someone's eyes watching me and realize that my chance had failed. I was afraid to find out that I was visible. I moved in a hurry. I felt like I was not walking on the ground anymore, but was floating above it. I was afraid that if I stopped for a second or if I turned around, I would immediately wake up. Everything that I was experiencing at the moment would collapse into ruins and turn back into endless fear and misery. I was so afraid it was just a dream.

I kept walking forward. The sky became lighter and the sun spread its rays to the ground. I finally began to distinguish the sounds of the earth. Somewhere near I heard the cows mooing; and the wind resumed. I crunched and broke the dried mud under my feet. I realized I was barefoot then, but I did not feel any discomfort. I was blown away by the ultimate glee. I just moved forward without knowing where I was going. I was carried by excitement along the dry and drought-parched surface.

I kept walking up the hill. I was in a hurry to meet my life, taken from me eight months ago.

June 7, 1995
Astrakhan, Russia

The woman was starting a new day, which would again be filled with pain and empty hopes. After eight long months of tragedy, severe pain dulled and faded and gave way to grief. It was like a cancer that would not heal but bled and oozed relentlessly. Looking up to the blue sky, the woman as always asked the Almighty for help and prayed to give her the strength to survive another day. Her savings were almost gone, and it was necessary to go back to work, see people, talk and smile. At the first opportunity, when the government allowed it, she would go to Chechnya and find her daughter herself.

The telephone rang. She quickly walked over to the phone and picked up the handle.

"Hello."

On the other end, an official-sounding man pronounced her name and asked to speak with her.

"Yes, it's me."

"This morning in Chechnya a girl pretending to be your daughter walked out of the wilderness into one of our troop encampments. Could you tell us any distinctive features of your daughter: scars, birthmarks..."

The voice kept talking, but the woman no longer heard him. She was swept away by a wave of ecstatic joy. She was sure that this girl was not just pretending to be her daughter. This *was* her daughter!

She screamed into the phone with a stuttering voice, as if she was afraid of being late with an answer. She was afraid that if she hesitated even a moment, the officer would hang up and this conversation would disappear as if it never happened. Tears streamed from her eyes, and she did not try to restrain them.

She screamed instead:

"Yes, yes, this is her! This is my daughter! She has two birthmarks..."

The woman was ready to rush to the meeting. Emotions overwhelmed her. Feelings of happiness and joy, which seemed to have left her eight months ago forever, were coming back. They came rushing at her and swallowed her.

Immediately she went to the train station and bought the next ticket to Dagestan, where a government officer would meet her at the train station and take her to see her daughter.

Nine hours of travel seemed like an eternity. She did not want to suppress her excitement - she wanted to hug the whole world and to share happiness with everyone. The sweetness of the euphoria overwhelmed her. She came out of the train compartment and stood at the half-open window in the corridor. A warm wind blew hard and did not let her eyes open. So she stood with her eyes closed, blown by the wind, holding on to the handrails and breathing the fresh air of freedom, remembering the sweet and heart-melting moments of the day.

Finally, they announced her station. She jumped out of the train onto the platform, almost on the fly and immediately found the officer in the loose crowd. She ran up to him and together they sat in a parked car nearby.

The officer was a pleasant young man with the interesting name of Venjamin. He beamed and slowly told her the story of her daughter. Despite her inner excitement, a pleasant languor enveloped the woman and she eagerly listened to every word uttered by the officer.

He told her a happy story about how her daughter went to the federal troops, located near the border of Dagestan. She walked barefoot, in a long blue dress, waving a white handkerchief as a flag of surrender. She was, of course, at first mistaken for a suicide bomber and seized. But it soon became clear who she was. Inside a military tank, she was brought to the border, to a safe area, and the General of the Army took her to his home. His wife and children were happy to offer her shower, food and clothes. She had spent the night peacefully and was now waiting to come home.

The woman was filled with the excitement and overwhelmed with happiness. With the officer, she climbed to the second floor and entered the flat of the General.

The woman stepped into a modest apartment and immediately saw the most very dear person on earth, and her favorite green eyes that glowed with excitement. They rushed into each other's arms, and without a word stood huddled together after their long separation, and silently wept tears of joy.

ABOUT THE AUTHOR

Elena Nikitina was born in the city of Astrakhan, Russia, during the time of the Soviet Union. In 1994, she was abducted by a Chechen gang, and taken to Grozny, the capital city of Chechnya. She survived the First Russian-Chechen War, eventually escaping an abandoned mountain village, and walking into the middle of a Russian army encampment while waving a white handkerchief. She immigrated to the United States and received political asylum.

Elena loves to hear from you. Contact her through her website:

www.GirlTaken.com.

Made in the USA
Lexington, KY
27 January 2018